INTERNET OF THINGS: PRINCIPLES AND MANAGEMENTS

AF569491

DR. K P MANIKANDAN

Copyright © Dr. K P Manikandan
All Rights Reserved.

ISBN 979-888546640-0

This book has been published with all efforts taken to make the material error-free after the consent of the author. However, the author and the publisher do not assume and hereby disclaim any liability to any party for any loss, damage, or disruption caused by errors or omissions, whether such errors or omissions result from negligence, accident, or any other cause.

While every effort has been made to avoid any mistake or omission, this publication is being sold on the condition and understanding that neither the author nor the publishers or printers would be liable in any manner to any person by reason of any mistake or omission in this publication or for any action taken or omitted to be taken or advice rendered or accepted on the basis of this work. For any defect in printing or binding the publishers will be liable only to replace the defective copy by another copy of this work then available.

Contents

Foreword

This book accumulates the best in class for the standards and the board of IoT of logical and down to earth research in the IoT ideal models to help society. The book first expects to examine and diagram different parts of elements and system of IoI. The creators then, at that point, examine how the IoT speak with bury network, sensor correspondences, implanted gadgets and furthermore cloud by which IoT can help for computerized wellbeing and gaining from modern perspectives.

The following piece of book examines specialized enhancements in the fields of safety and security. The book additionally covers Smart undertakings modern and social government assistance. The book is focused on towards propelling specialists, academicians and industry research experts who are presently working in the area of science and innovation either straightforwardly or by implication to help normal masses.

Dr.V.NIRMAL KANNAN
Principal
VSB Engineering College
Karur

Preface

The Internet of Things (IoT) is a multi-layered, interconnected arrangement of frameworks made up out of an assorted of equipment gadgets, programming applications, information principles, correspondence standards, and cloud administrations. It very well may be precarious to confront these difficulties with your own IoT project. Programming the Internet of Things is a book that will kick you off on your IoT standards and the executive's excursion and tell you the best way to make the Internet of Things work as a designer.

This book will take you through a coordinated IoT standards and the board utilizing different genuine applications. In every part, creators give a short prologue to that section's subject alongside some supportive foundation material, which will incorporate some appropriate definitions. I'll likewise sum up why the subject is significant and what you can hope to learn, and you can decide to execute also.

In the event that you study and gain proficiency with the ideas in this book, you will be en route to turning into the uncommon "force of IoT" who can say for sure how things work and how to fix them when they break. Our point is to introduce the key ideas in manners that you will see as valuable immediately. You will likewise be ready to dive further, concentrating on such themes as IoT: Introduction, Features and Framework of IoT, Communication Protocols, IoT : Embedded Devices, IoT: Projects, IoT: Management and Security and wellbeing.

Acknowledgements

Most importantly, we express my gratitude to our folks for giving us an exceptionally pleasant climate for doing this task. We wish to communicate our genuine gratitude to the **Chairman Shri.V.S.BALSAMY** for his undertaking in instructing us in this head foundation.

We wish to communicate our appreciation and thankfulness to Institutional Head, **Dr.V.NIRMAL KANNAN** and second in command **Mr.T.S.KIRUBASANKAR** for their support and earnest direction.

Our genuine gratitude to all the school personnel of **V.S.B Engineering College** and our companions for their assistance in the fruitful culmination of this task work.

At long last we bow before God, the all-powerful who consistently had a superior arrangement for us. We give our commendation and wonder to Almighty God for effective fruition of this undertaking.

Prologue

This book assembles the best in class for the standards and the executives of IoT of logical and down to earth research in the IoT ideal models to help society. The book first plans to examine and diagram different parts of elements and system of Iot.. The creators then, at that point, talk about how the IoT speak with buries network, sensor interchanges, installed gadgets and furthermore cloud by which IoT can help for computerized wellbeing and gaining from modern angles. The following piece of book examines specialized upgrades in the fields of safety and security. The book additionally covers Smart undertakings modern and social government assistance. The book is focused on towards propelling undergrad, graduate, and post alumni understudies, scientists, academicians, policymakers, different government authorities, NGOs, and industry research experts who are right now working in the area of science and innovation either straightforwardly or by implication to help normal masses.

Today the Internet has become pervasive, has contacted pretty much every side of the globe, and is influencing human existence in impossible ways. We are currently entering a period of much more inescapable network where an extremely wide assortment of machines will be associated with the web.

In like manner speech, the Internet of Things alludes to another sort of world where practically every one of the gadgets and apparatuses that we use are associated with an organization. We can utilize them cooperatively to accomplish complex undertakings that require a serious level of insight. For this insight and interconnection, IoT gadgets are outfitted with implanted sensors, actuators, processors, and handsets. IoT is anything but a solitary innovation; rather it is an agglomeration of different advancements that cooperates pair. Sensors and actuators are gadgets, which help in associating with the actual climate. The information gathered by the sensors must be put away and handled insightfully to get valuable inductions from it. So the Internet of Things (IoT) is certainly not an implausible idea; it's in all over the place. Conventional installed frameworks are joined with little remote miniature sensors, control frameworks with mechanization, and different parts to shape a monstrous foundation. Remote correspondence, miniature electromechanical gadgets, and the Internet have all been utilized to make new things on the Internet. It's an organization of organization protests that might be gotten to by means of the Internet, with everything having its own one of a kind recognizable proof. The objective of an Internet of Things application is to make things shrewd without requiring human contribution.

CHAPTER ONE

IoT: Introduction

Introduction

Internet of Things (IoT) is an organization of actual articles or individuals called "things" that are inserted with programming, gadgets, organization, and sensors that permits these items to gather and trade information. The objective of IoT is to reach out to web network from standard gadgets like PC, portable, tablet to moderately imbecilic gadgets like a toaster oven.

IoT makes basically everything "brilliant," by further developing parts of our existence with the force of information assortment, AI calculation, and organizations. The thing in IoT can likewise be an individual with a diabetes screen embed, a creature with GPS beacons, and so forth This IoT instructional exercise for fledglings covers every one of the Basics of IoT.

History of IoT

- 1970- The actual idea of connected devices was proposed
- 1990- John Romkey created a toaster which could be turned on/off over the Internet
- 1995- Siemens introduced the first cellular module built for M2M
- 1999- The term “Internet of Things” was used by Kevin Ashton during his work at P&G which became widely accepted
- 2004 – The term was mentioned in famous publications like the Guardian, Boston Globe, and Scientific American
- 2005-UN’s International Telecommunications Union (ITU) published its first report on this topic.
- 2008- The Internet of Things was born
- 2011- Gartner, the market research company, include “The Internet of Things” technology in their research

Working Environment

The whole IoT measure begins with the actual gadgets like cell phones, smart watches, electronic apparatuses like TV, Washing Machine which assists you with speaking with the

IoT stage.

Presently in this IoT instructional exercise, four major parts of an IoT framework:

1) **Sensors/Devices:** Sensors or gadgets are a key part that assists you with gathering live information from the general climate. This information might have different degrees of intricacies. It very well may be a straightforward temperature checking sensor, or it could be as the video feed.

2) **Connectivity:** All the gathered information is shipped off a cloud framework. The sensors ought to be associated with the cloud utilizing different modes of interchanges. These correspondence mediums incorporate versatile or satellite organizations, Bluetooth, WI-FI, WAN, and so forth

3) **Data Processing:** Once that information is gathered, and it gets to the cloud, the product performs handling on the assembled information. This cycle can be simply taking a look at the temperature, perusing on gadgets like AC or radiators. Be that as it may, it can here and there additionally be extremely mind boggling like distinguishing objects, utilizing PC vision on record.

4) **User Interface:** The data should be accessible to the end-client here and there which can be accomplished by setting off alerts on their telephones or sending them notice through email or instant message. The client some of the time may require an interface which effectively looks at their IoT framework. For instance, the client has a

camera introduced in his home. He needs to get to video recording and every one of the feeds with the assistance of a web server.

Be that as it may, it's not generally single direction correspondence. Contingent upon the IoT application and intricacy of the framework, the client may likewise have the option to play out an activity which might make falling impacts.

For instance, if a client recognizes any progressions in the temperature of the cooler, with the assistance of IoT innovation the client ought to ready to change the temperature with the assistance of their cell phone.

IoT Applications

A gadget might have different sorts of sensors which plays out numerous errands separated from detecting. Model, A cell phone is a gadget which has numerous sensors like GPS, camera however your cell phone can't detect these things.

- **Store Thermostats:** Helps you to save asset on warming bills by realizing your use designs.
- Associated Cars: IoT helps vehicle organizations handle charging, leaving, protection, and other related stuff naturally.
- **Movement Trackers:** Helps you to catch pulse design, calorie use, action levels, and skin temperature on your wrist.
- **Keen Outlets:** Remotely turn any gadget on or off. It likewise permits you to follow a gadget's energy even out and get custom notices straightforwardly into your

cell phone.

- **Stopping Sensors:** IoT innovation assists to the clients with distinguishing the ongoing accessibility of parking spots on their telephone.
- **Interface Health:** The idea of an associated medical care framework works with constant wellbeing checking and patient consideration. It helps in further developed clinical dynamic dependent on understanding information.

Savvy City: Smart city offers a wide range of utilization cases which incorporate traffic the executives to water appropriation, squander the board, and so forth

Savvy Home: Smart home embodies the network inside your homes. It incorporates smoke alarms, home apparatuses, lights, windows, entryway locks, and so on

Savvy Supply Chain: Helps you continuously following of merchandise while they are out and about, or getting providers to trade stock data.

Difficulties of Internet of Things (IoT)

At present IoT is confronted with many difficulties, for example,

- Deficient testing and refreshing
- Concern in regards to information security and protection
- Programming intricacy
- Information volumes and translation
- Incorporation with AI and computerization
- Gadgets require a steady force supply which is troublesome

- Collaboration and short-range correspondence
- Benefits of IoT
- Key advantages of IoT innovation are as per the following:

Specialized Optimization: IoT innovation helps a ton in further developing advancements and improving them. Model, with IoT, a producer can gather information from different vehicle sensors. The producer breaks down them to work on its plan and make them more proficient.

Data Collection: Traditional information assortment has its impediments and its plan for aloof use. IoT works with prompt activity on information.

Decreased Waste: IoT offers continuous data prompting viable dynamic and the board of assets. For instance, if a producer discovers an issue in numerous motors, he can follow the assembling plan of those motors and tackles this issue with the assembling belt.

Customer Engagement: IoT permits you to further develop client experience by recognizing issues and working on the interaction.

Detriments IoT

Presently, how about we see a portion of the impediments of IoT in this Internet of Things instructional exercise:

Security: IoT innovation makes a biological system of associated gadgets. Notwithstanding, during this interaction, the framework might offer little validation control regardless of adequate safety efforts.

Protection: The utilization of IoT, uncovered a generous measure of individual information, in outrageous detail, without the client's dynamic support. This makes bunches of security issues.

Adaptability: There is a gigantic concern in regards to the adaptability of an IoT framework. It is primarily viewing coordinating with one more framework as there are numerous assorted frameworks engaged with the interaction.

Intricacy: The plan of the IoT framework is additionally very convoluted. Besides, it's arrangement and support additionally not extremely simple.

Consistence: IoT has its own arrangement of rules and guidelines. Notwithstanding, in light of its intricacy, the undertaking of consistence is very difficult.

IoT Best Practices

Presently find out with regards to Best practices for IoT in this Internet of Things instructional exercise.

- Plan items for unwavering quality and security
- Utilize solid validation and security conventions
- Handicap insignificant administrations
- Guarantee Internet-oversaw, and IoT the executives center points and administrations are gotten
- Energy effective calculations ought to be intended for the framework to be dynamic longer.

Advantages and Disadvantages of (IoT)

Any technology available today has not reached to its 100 % capability. It always has a gap to go. So, we can verbally express that Internet of Things has a paramount technology in a world that can avail other technologies to reach its precise and consummate 100 % capability as well. Let's take a look over the major, advantages, and disadvantages of the Internet of Things.

Advantages of IoT

Internet of things facilitates the several advantages in day-to-day life in the business sector. Some of its benefits are given below:

- **Efficient resource utilization:** If we ken the functionality and the way that how each contrivance works we definitely increase the efficient resource utilization as well as monitor natural resources.
- **Minimize human effort:** As the contrivances of IoT interact and communicate with each other and do lot of task for us, then they minimize the human effort.
- **Save time:** As it minimizes the human effort then it definitely preserves out time. Time is the primary factor which can preserve through IoT platform.
- **Improve security:** Now, if we have a system that all these things are interconnected then we can make the system more secure and efficient.

Disadvantages of IoT

As the Internet of things facilitates a set of benefits, it withal engenders a paramount set of challenges. Some of the IoT challenges are given below:

- **Security:** As the IoT systems are interconnected and communicate over networks. The system offers little control despite any security measures, and it can be lead the sundry kinds of network attacks.
- **Privacy:** Even without the active participation on the utilize, the IoT system provides substantial personal data in maximum detail.
- **Complexity:** The designing, developing, and maintaining and enabling the sizably voluminous technology to IoT system is quite intricate.

Understanding IoT utilizing Cases Studies

The ascension of IoT enabled applications has made businesses develop high-efficient and keenly intellective applications. Let's understand the accommodations an IoT software development company can provide. Majorly it is relegated into two groups:

1. Industrial IoT (IIoT)

The Industrial IoT refers to the application of IoT in industrial applications, including manufacturing and energy management. Nowadays, most of the industries are shifting their focus towards the adoption of (machine-to-machine) M2M communication to achieve wireless automation and control. This vicissitude in technology with the emergence of cloud and cognate technologies like analytics and ML can avail businesses achieve incipient heights in automation and can engender advanced business models that boost revenue and business can invest their time in more strategic work.

2. Consumer IoT

This second type IOT application is consumer IoT that can connect billions of physical contrivances via the cyber world and shared which accumulates information from multiple connected contrivances such as smartphones, astute wearables and other keenly intellective home appliances.

IoT as a technology has engendered wonders for most of the business and its applications are growing at a more expeditious rate. Let's take an optical canvassing of some of the IoT use cases of the genuine world.

•Smart Homes and Astute Cities

How facile life would be if we can interact with home appliances and control them through voice. The appliances can automatically sense the environment and operate accordingly without any human intervention like dimming the living room lights, setting the thermostat to a cozy temperature, etc. These are some of the mundane use cases of this technology which are availing humans build astute homes with incremented efficiency of contrivances and abbreviated costs of maintenance.The concept of inducing IoT in Keenly Intellective Cities to achieve an energy-efficient and environmentally convivial infrastructure was the prime motto. These IoT contrivances exhibited authentic-time information on the air quality detected by sensors across a city and soothsay values for the upcoming days, which will contribute towards optimizing traffic with sensor-predicated traffic light control and astute parking. You can read IoT predicated Perspicacious City Case Study here.

•Fitness Trackers, Keenly Intellective Watches and other Wearables

Fitness trackers are another vital example of IoT enabled contrivances that quantify the number of steps taken in a day by an individual. But people are probing for options where the data can be stored in their smartphones for tracking and analysis. So to meet this requisite smartwatches are available in the market which makes a seamless connection with the smartphones to track, manage, and secure their sensitive health data through advanced mobile apps. There are supplementally some other wearable contrivances available such as voice-operated headphones, kids-tracker, etc.

•Autonomous and Connected Vehicles

Self-driving Cars or Driverless Cars is a solid amalgamation of sensors, cameras, radar and AI in a single application. These Driverless cars are embedded with all these functionalities including ranging LIDAR that captures and stores information on road conditions, weather, driving ordinant dictations and amassed data averts potential road accidents.

•*Drones or Unmanned Aerial Conveyance (UAV)*

It has availed many businesses such as cinematographers and photographers to simplify their quotidian operations. Drones have availed record stunning landscapes, oil rig workers to consummate full rig inspections expeditiously and avail e-commerce companies to distribute goods at customer doorstep. Along with this, drones are withal used to avail public safety units in rescue missions. Drones are supplementally part of surveillance systems for security purposes.

•*Supply Chain IoT*

This enabled contrivances are withal utilized in the Supply chain sector to amend communication and enhance the distribution process. Without the utilization of IoT in the supply chain, it was getting tremendously involute and equivocal. E-commerce companies utilize the supply chain process to track customer orders. The magnification in customer requisites evolves and thus the products have to be procured, shipped and distributed on time with the routes coordinated accordingly. In replication to this, companies are engendering connected enterprise systems and utilizing data modeling as a consequential part of data management strategy.

Businesses supplemental incline to utilize low powered IoT contrivances to track products throughout the supply chain and examine the quality with essential contributing factors such as temperature, vibration and container apertures, etc.

5. The More Tenebrous Side Of Iot Technology

Security is the most sizably voluminous concern in IoT-enabled connected contrivances. Contrivances embedded with sensors accumulate profoundly sensitive data in many cases which are prone to get hacked due to poor security measures in IoT technology.

Researchers have discovered that around 100,000 webcams can be hacked facilely because of a lack of security. For a few connected contrivances designed for children like Smart watches are vulnerably susceptible to threats of getting hacked. The hackers can facilely spy on conversations, track the utilize location and communicate with users as well. With such high jeopardizes, businesses can't afford to implement IoT in their subsisting business plans. Supplementally, if there is ascension in the utilization of IIOT then the potential risk of getting hacked elevates and the security of information is disputable. So the IoT with felicitous security measures will make it the most used technology in all the areas.

6. The Final Takedown

In today's connected world where contrivances are more in touch than humans, the definition of staying connected is different now. We have visually perceived how IoT as a technology innovation has transformed the way businesses work. With the prelude of IoT in most of the businesses, they feel more connected and optimized. Though there are cost concerns, connectivity issues, acceptance, and security concerns, yet the cessation goal seems more promising than afore. With the magnification in the number of connected contrivances, the working environment will become the commencement and automated by accepting imperfections of security and privacy trade-offs.

CHAPTER TWO

Features and Framework of IOT

The Internet of Things is the set of technologies that make objects “smart”, so that these act and communicate with us or with other objects, apprising us of what transpires nearby.

The most paramount features of IoT on which it works are connectivity, analyzing, integrating, active engagement, and many more. Some of them are listed below:

1. Astuteness

IoT comes with the accumulation of algorithms and computation, software & hardware that makes it perspicacious. Ambient perspicacity in IoT enhances its capabilities which facilitate the things to respond in a keenly intellective way to a particular situation and fortifies them in carrying out categorical tasks. In spite of all the popularity of perspicacious technologies, perspicacity in IoT is only concerned as an expedient of interaction between contrivances, while utilize and contrivance interaction are achieved by standard input methods and graphical utilize interface.

Connectivity: Connectivity refers to establish an opportune connection between all the things of IoT to IoT platform it may be server or cloud. After connecting the IoT contrivances, it requires a high speed messaging between the contrivances and cloud to enable reliable, secure and bi-directional communication.

Analyzing: After connecting all the germane things, it comes to genuine-time analyzing the data accumulated and utilize them to build efficacious business astuteness. If we have a good insight into data amassed from all these things, then we call our system has an astute system.

Integrating: IoT integrating the sundry models to ameliorate the utilizer experience as well.

Artificial Astuteness: IoT makes things keenly intellective and enhances life through the utilization of data. For example, if we have a coffee machine whose beans have going to culminate, then the coffee machine it orders the coffee beans of your cull from the retailer.

Heterogeneity in Internet of Things as one of the key characteristics. Contrivances in IoT are predicated on different hardware platforms and networks and can interact with other contrivances or accommodation platforms through different networks. IoT architecture should fortify direct network connectivity between heterogeneous networks. The key design requisites for heterogeneous things and their environments in IoT are scalabilities, modularity, extensibility and interoperability.

Security: IoT contrivances are naturally vulnerably susceptible to security threats. As we gain efficiencies, novel experiences, and other benefits from the IoT, it would be a mistake to forget about security concerns associated with it. There is a high caliber of transparency and privacy issues with IoT. It is paramount to secure the endpoints, the networks, and the data that is transferred across all of it signifies engendering a security paradigm.

Sensing: The sensor contrivances utilized in IoT technologies detect and quantify any transmutation in the environment and report on their status. IoT technology brings passive networks to active networks. Without sensors, there could not hold an efficacious or veritable IoT environment.

Scaling: The number of contrivances that need to be managed and that communicate with each other will be much more immensely colossal than the contrivances connected to the current Internet. The management of data engendered from these contrivances and their interpretation for application purposes becomes more critical. Gartner (2015) substantiates the brobdingnagian scale of IoT in the estimated report where it verbally expressed that 5.5 million incipient things will get connected every day and 6.4 billion connected things will be in utilization ecumenical in 2016, which is up by 30 percent from 2015. The report additionally forecasts that the number of connected contrivances will reach 20.8 billion by 2020.

Active Engagement: IoT makes the connected technology, product, or accommodations to active engagement between each other.

Endpoint Management: It is paramount to be the endpoint management of all the IoT system otherwise, it makes the consummate failure of the system. For example, if a coffee machine itself order the coffee beans when it goes to culminate but what transpires when it orders the beans from a retailer and we are not present at home for a few days, it leads to the failure of the IoT system. So, there must be a desideratum for endpoint management.

Today, the Internet has become a major part of the world. It finds application in every corner of the globe.

With the incrementing utilization of the Internet, more appliances and contrivances are now being connected to the web, composing the 'Internet of Things,' commonly kenned by its acronym 'IoT'. The IoT is not just a simple technology. It is an involute framework that includes several different technologies, designed to collaborate in tandem. In this article, you will learn what the IoT framework is in detail, as well as the Open source IoT frameworks.

What is IoT Framework?

Mundanely, when sizably voluminous data is being engendered and transmitted across a number of contrivances, there has to be a categorical point where everything is amassed and amalgamated.

This concrete point is very essential in a network, as it amalgamates all data, making it possible to understand the data being engendered.

However, the smooth transmission and generation of data don't just transpire. Rather, it is customarily made possible by the Internet of Things Framework, (IoT framework). So, just what is IoT framework?

The Internet of Things (IoT) Framework can be described as being an ecosystem, comprising of several connected contrivances that communicate with each other, over the Internet. These connected contrivances customarily work to transfer and sense data over the Internet, while requiring very little human intervention.

The IoT framework is what makes it possible for the connected contrivances to have smooth communication over the Internet. It is no wonder, then, that it is referred to as the 'Internet of Things' framework, or in other words, the framework that facilitates the interaction of 'Things' (contrivances) over the Internet.

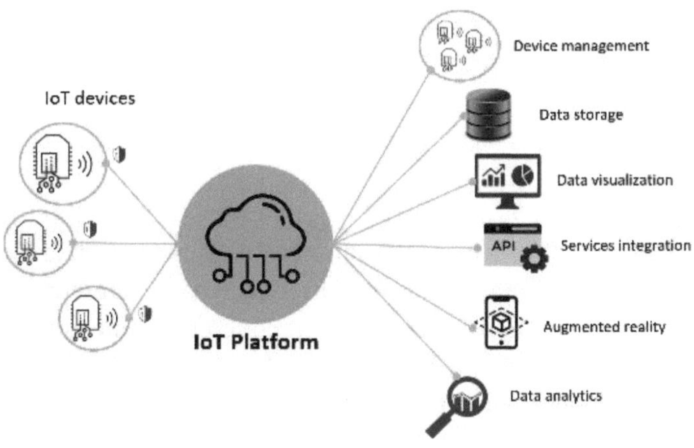

Fig.1. IoT Framework

IoT Framework Overview

The IoT framework is a very consequential element of technology in the modern world, finding application in virtually every sector. For instance, one of the major applications of the IoT is in the designing of keenly intellective homes.

The IoT framework concept is withal applied in the designing of different physical objects, such as thermostats, electrical contrivances, security and alarm systems, as well as vending machines, among many other objects.

The IoT Framework

Exordium

Today, the Internet has become a major part of the world. It finds application in every corner of the globe. With the incrementing utilization of the Internet, more appliances and contrivances are now being connected to the web, composing the 'Internet of Things,' commonly kenned by its acronym 'IoT'. The IoT is not just a simple technology. It is an involute framework that includes several different technologies, designed to collaborate in tandem. In this article, you will learn what the IoT framework is in detail, as well as the Open source IoT frameworks.

What is IoT Framework?

Customarily, when astronomically immense data is being engendered and transmitted across a number of contrivances, there has to be a concrete point where everything is accumulated and cumulated.

This concrete point is very essential in a network, as it amalgamates all data, making it possible to understand the data being engendered.

However, the smooth transmission and generation of data don't just transpire. Rather, it is conventionally made possible by the Internet of Things Framework, (IoT framework). So, just what is IoT framework?

The Internet of Things (IoT) Framework can be described as being an ecosystem, comprising of several connected contrivances that communicate with each other, over the Internet. These connected contrivances customarily work to transfer and sense data over the Internet, while requiring very little hIoT Testing Framework

The IoT framework is gaining a plethora of popularity recently and is even believed to have the highest chances of becoming the most sizably voluminous software development of all time. This is why it has become consequential to test this software and its contrivances, so as to ascertain that it not only offers the best accommodations but withal meets the highest quality standards. This type of testing is what is referred to as IoT testing.

Why Internet of Things Testing?

IoT testing is very consequential in the field of computer networking and software development. The following are the 3 main benefits of IoT testing;

1) Ameliorates Engagement

IoT testing framework works to ascertain that the terminus-utilizer gets the best and most facile experience, for all the channels, such as connected contrivances and mobiles.

2) Future-Proofs Businesses

IoT testing framework ascertains the security, best performance and interoperability of a business, which in turn accommodates as a Future-Proof for the business.

3) Expedite Time-to-Market

IoT testing framework does this by leveraging early automation, hence, ascertaining an expedited time-to-market.

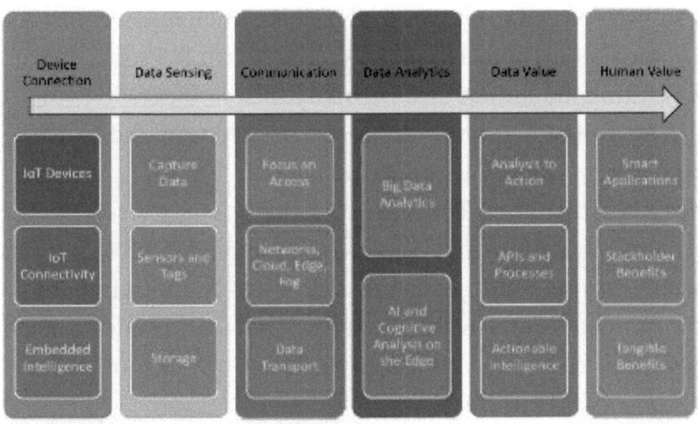

Fig.2. Types of Testing Across the IoT Framework

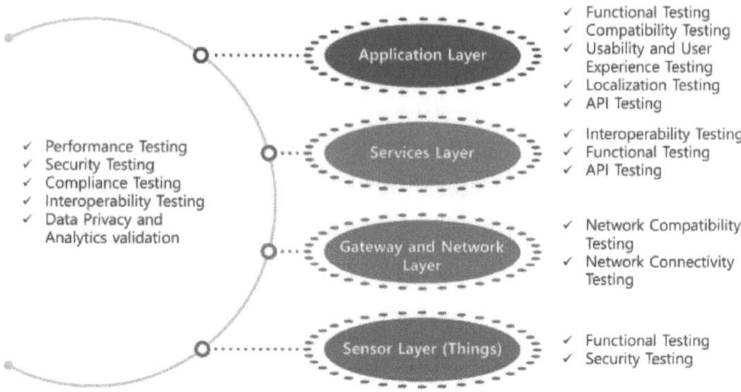

Fig.2.(a). Types of Testing on different Layers

The IoT framework is a very consequential element of technology in the modern world, finding application in virtually every sector, For instance, one of the major applications of the IoT is in the designing of astute homes.

The IoT framework concept is withal applied in the designing of different physical objects, such as thermostats, electrical contrivances, security and alarm systems, as well as vending machines, among many other objects.

The following types of tests are recommended to be done across the IoT framework:

1) Performance Testing

Performing testing is conventionally conducted so as to determine how expeditious the functioning of a communication network model is. This testing additionally looks into the computation capabilities of the internal part of the software system.

This IoT Performance testing framework is customarily done in 3 levels:

- The Network and Gateway level, which involves protocols such as HTTP and MQTT
- The System level
- The Application level

A good example of Performance IoT testing is the verification of replication time against a concrete bench-marked time, with concretely defined connectivity settings.

2) Security Testing

The security testing aspect of the IoT framework deals with security elements, such as the bulwark of data, as well as encryption and decryption. It is aimed at providing integrated security to connected contrivances, and additionally to the networks and cloud accommodations on which the contrivances are connected.

Some variables that mostly cause security threats in IoT are sensor networks, applications that work to accumulate data, and interfaces. Ergo, it is highly recommended that security testing be done at the contrivance and protocol level, since quandaries can facilely be detected and solved at this caliber.

An example of security testing is the verification of no unauthorized access to a particular contrivance.

3) Compatibility Testing

The main purport of compatibility testing is to validate all the possible functional coalescences of contrivances, their hardware, protocol and software versions, as well as operating systems, such as the mobile OS versions.

This compatibility testing is conventionally done in two levels:

- The Application layer

- The Network layer

A good example of compatibility testing is verifying that particular IoT software fortifies a given set of contrivances.

4) End-Utilizer Application Testing

The Terminus-utilizer application testing takes into consideration the utilizer experience, as well as the usability and functionality of the IoT application.

An example of this IoT testing framework is the verification of an IoT application, so as to ascertain that it includes all required features, and in a good working condition as well.

5) Contrivance Interoperability Testing

This type of testing aims to assess the interoperability of protocols and contrivances, compared with varying standards and designations.

In other words, in an IoT framework, the contrivance interoperability testing is conducted so as to verify the connectivity of all contrivances and protocols.

This testing is conventionally done in the Accommodation layer. This is because the accommodation layer provides the most conducive environment for this testing, that is; a platform that is communicable, programmable and operable.

Python IoT Framework

The Python programming language is the most recommended for analysis of data in IoT framework. It is a simple language and offers facile readability and deployment.

The python IoT framework additionally has an immensely colossal number of libraries, which designates that it can do a lot with few codes. Consequently, if you deal with dataintensive applications, then you would do well to utilize the python IoT Framework.

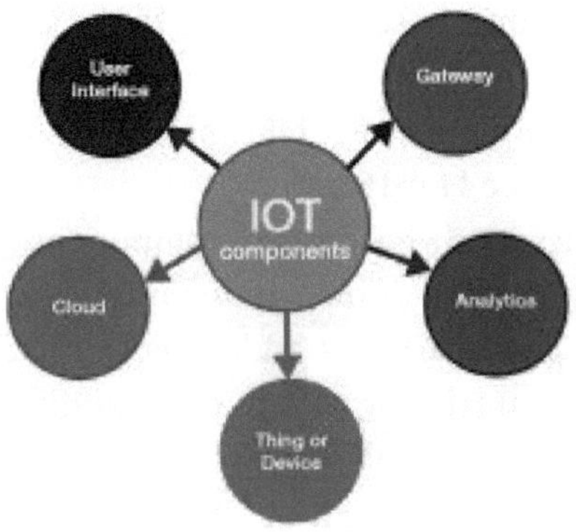

Fig.3.Open Source IoT Frameworks

In order to understand what an IoT framework open source is, consider these three facts;

1) Every consumer wishes that they can utilize any technology contrivance of their cull, without being circumscribed or coerced to utilize contrivances from just one particular vendor (for instance, some astute-watches require that they are paired with only smart phones from the same vendor).

2) All dealers of IoT contrivances wish that the integration of their contrivances can be made much more facile, and even possible with a sizably voluminous number of different technology ecosystems.

3) Those who develop applications wish that they could fortify many different contrivances, which do not require any developed vendor-concrete codes. The Open source framework is a solution to all the above challenges. It sanctions for such levels of scale to be achieved, and withal high flexibility levels. Most of the IoT framework open

sources are in liberty to download and can be installed and launched quite facilely. The Cyber World offers an astronomically immense variety of open sources for the IoT Framework.

Major Components of IoT Framework

1) Contrivance Hardware

The contrivance hardware component of the IoT framework requires some rudimental cognizance on architecture. The utilizer is additionally required to have a conception on the working of the different micro-controllers, as well the sensors.Examples of hardware contrivances that form part of this IoT framework component are sensors, micro-controllers and controllers.

2) Contrivance Software

In order for the contrivance software of the IoT framework to function felicitously, the included inscribing applications are required to configure the controller, and then operate them remotely. The utilize is required to have a rudimental understanding of how an API works inside the micro-controllers, as well how libraries are customarily made for programming.

3) Communication and Cloud Platform

The cloud platform is one of the most crucial components of the IoT framework. It calls for the rudimental erudition of all communication, whether wireless or wired. The utilizer is additionally required to have a good understanding of IoT integration, as well as the working of the cloud technology. In summary, we can verbally express the communication and Cloud Platform of the IoT Framework is where all communications transpire.

4) Cloud Application

The cloud application is a type of software program, which mainly consists of components that can be accessed quite more facile and more expeditious. These components can be either local or even cloud-predicated. The cloud application works to ameliorate the system, such that its maximum potential is realized. In other words, the cloud application can be defined as the indicted application of an IoT framework, which binds all the local hardware contrivances, as well as the cloud-predicated contrivances.

IoT- Decision Framework

The IoT decision framework lays out a method for developing a strong IoT product strategy. The Internet of Things decision framework is all about making strategic decisions. The IoT Decision Framework assists us in identifying areas where we must make judgments and maintains consistency across all of our strategic business, technical, and other decisions.

Because the product or service communicates through networks, the IoT decision framework is considerably more significant, as it passes through five different layers of technological complexity.

1. Hardware of the device
2. Software for the Device
3. Communications
4. Platform for the Cloud
5. Application of the Cloud

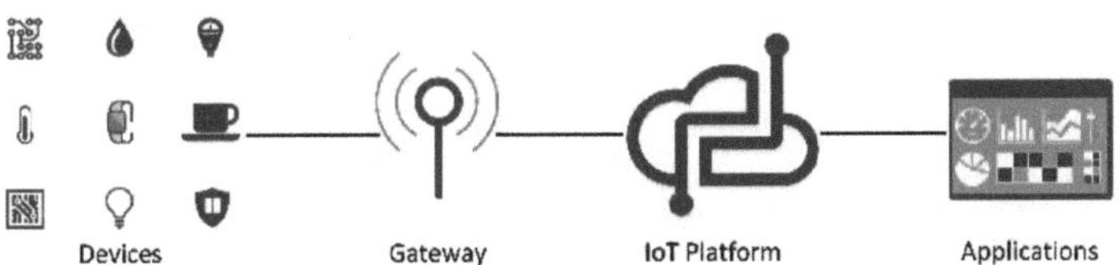

Fig.4.Area of Determination

Any IoT product must consider six critical choice areas, according to the IoT decision framework. These are the decision-making areas:

1. The User's Perspective (UX)
2. Data
3. Business
4. Technology
5. Security
6. Rules and Regulations

At each stage of the IoT Technology Stack, each of these decision areas is assessed. The User Experience will be assessed in terms of device hardware, software, and other factors in order to deliver a better user experience. Then, in the Data Decision Area, we must investigate data implications for all levels of the IoT Technology Stack.Differenctween JDK, JRE, and JVM

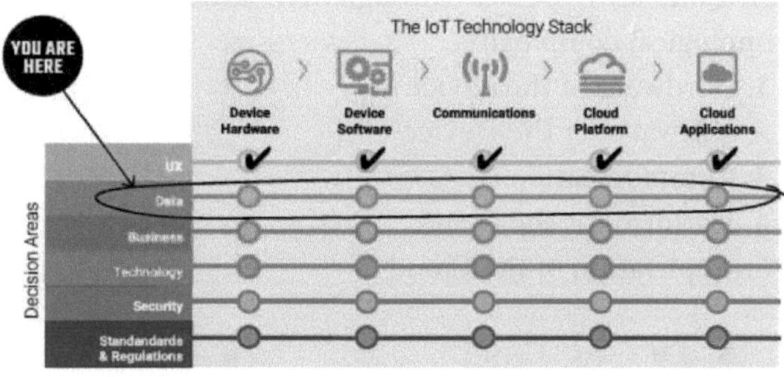

Fig.5. The IoT Decision Framework's Decision Area

Let's take a closer look at each of the Decision Areas in the IoT Decision Framework:

1. User Experience Decision Area: In this area, we focus on who the users are, what their needs are, and how to give a fantastic experience at each step of the IoT stack without getting bogged down in technical specifics.
2. Data Decision Area: In this area, we plan the overall data strategy, such as data flow throughout the complete IoT stack, to meet the needs of the users.
3. Business Decision Area: We make a decision based on the preceding decision area about how a product or service will become financially viable. The costs of providing services are monetized at each level of the IoT Stack.
4. Technology Decision Area: We work with the technology for each layer in this area to make the ultimate solution easier.
5. Security Decision Area: After completing the technology deployment, it is critical to determine and offer security at each stage of the IoT Stack.
6. IoT Decision Area: In the final stage of the IoT Decision Area, we determine the product or service standards and regulations that will affect your product at each layer of the IoT Stack.

Architecture for the Internet of Things: On the Internet of Things (IoT) architecture, there is no globally established unique or standard consensus. Their functional area and solutions differ from their IoT architecture. The IoT architectural technology, on the other hand, is made up of four fundamental components.

IoT Architecture Components

- Sensors/Devices
- Networks and Gateways
- Management/Cloud Service Layer
- Application
- Stages of IoT Solutions Architecture

There are several layers of IoT built upon the capability and performance of IoT elements that provides the optimal solution to the business enterprises and culminate-users. The IoT architecture is a fundamental way to design the sundry elements of IoT, so that it can distribute accommodations over the networks and accommodate the desiderata for the future.

Following are the primary stages (layers) of IoT that provides the solution for IoT architecture.

1.Sensors/Actuators: Sensors or Actuators are the contrivances that are able to emit, accept and process data over the network. These sensors or actuators may be connected either through wired or wireless. This contains GPS, Electrochemical, Gyroscope, RFID, etc. Most of the sensors need connectivity through sensors gateways. The connection of sensors or actuators can be through a Local Area Network (LAN) or Personal Area Network.

2.Gateways and Data Acquisition: As the sizably voluminous numbers of data are engendered by this sensors and actuators need the high-speed Gateways and Networks to transfer the data. This network can be of type Local Area Network (LAN such as WiFi, Ethernet, etc.), Wide Area Network (WAN such as GSM, 5G, etc.).

3.Edge IT: Edge in the IoT Architecture is the hardware and software gateways that analyze and pre-process the data afore transferring it to the cloud. If the data read from the sensors and gateways are not transmuted from its anterior reading value then it does not transfer over the cloud, this preserves the data utilized.

4. Data center/ Cloud: The Data Center or Cloud comes under the Management Accommodations which process the information through analytics, management of contrivance and security controls. Contiguous to this security controls and contrivance management the cloud transfer the data to the terminus users application such as Retail, Healthcare, Emergency, Environment, and Energy, etc.

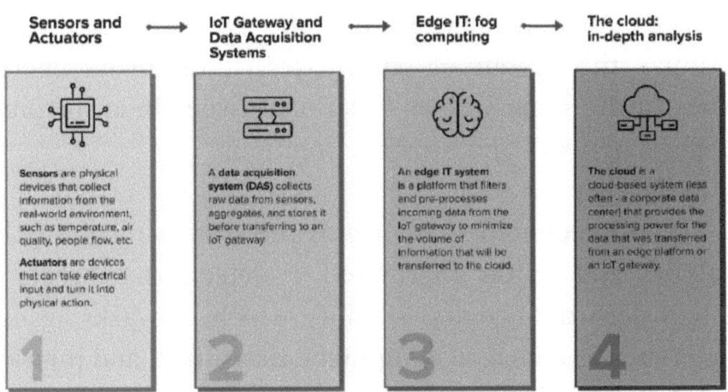

Fig. 6. Stages of IoT Architecture

IoT Energy Domain

The Cyber World of Things plays a vital role in the field of energy management and regulation. The term utilized for that is Perspicacious Energy System. IoT applications monitor a wide variety of energy control function to residential and commercial use.

Residential Energy

As technology is incrementing day by day, it additionally raises the cost of energy. Consumers probe the way through which they can abbreviate and control the energy cost. IoT provides a mature way to analyze and optimize the utilization of the contrivance as well as the entire system of a domicile. It may be transmuting the contrivance setting, simply switching on/off or dimming lights to optimize energy use.

Commercial Energy

Wastage of energy widely impacts any business enterprises in their cost of engenderment. IoT provides a concrete way for monitoring and maintaining a low cost and high caliber of care. IoT system provides a vigorous betokens of managing the consumption cost of energy and optimize the output of enterprises. It discovers energy issues in the same way as functional issues in an involute business network and provides solutions.

Reliability

The IoT technology ascertains the system reliability by analytics and action distributed. It detects the threats of system performance and stability which bulwarks against losses such as damaged equipment, downtime, and injuries.

IoT Biometrics Domain

IoT plays a vital role in the Biometrics security system such as a dactylogram system, voice apperception system, ocular perceiver scanner system etc.

Now, a biometric system is something that we always encounter in our circadian life. We always either utilize a dactylogram sensor or an ocular perceiver-scanning system, depends on organization to organization.

Let's verbalize about the dactylogram scanner system and how these systems work. Now, when a person presents its finger on the dactylogram scanner it scans the dactylogram and considers this as a component of an enrollment process. From this dactylogram template, the contrivance extracts certain key features which make different from others and stores it into a database. After that, every time the same person place its finger on the top of this dactylogram scanner, it engenders a template and compares this with all the templates that are present in the database. If it matches to correspondingly let's verbally express giving that person an attendance or sanctions him to access a door, if it does not then it raises a vigilant.

This biometric system can be dactylogram or ocular perceiver scanning or it could be a cumulation of both. Voice apperception system is additionally one of the key products in the biometric domain.

Security Camera & Door Unlock System

The Security Camera and a Door unlock system is something that is quite intriguing IoT application. The phenomena of its working process are briefly mentioned here.

How does this system work?

Here, we place a camera on the top foot of the door which in turn clicks the photo of a person who comes into frame. Now, this photo is sent to an analytical system which in turn compares this with all the photos it possesses to identify whether to let the utilizer open the door or not.

Now, if it does not find the photo of that person then it can notify the concern that a person is endeavoring to access this door would you relish to sanction this person? or would you relish to gainsay the access to this person?

Conventionally, the Security Camera and a Door unlock system is utilized in the areas where you have highly sensitive information stored. Another utilization of the security camera and door unlock system can be at our homes when we optate to identify who peregrinates to our abode when we are not there and either decide to give them access to our habitation or not.

IoT in Astute Home and Perspicacious City Application

Implementing IoT system in home and city leads them to become as perspicacious home and perspicacious city. Perspicacious home or keenly intellective city make life quite more facile and more astute.

A keenly intellective home system can be something that makes our life quite facile. Starting from energy management where the potency controls system in the AC appliances where we utilize the thermostat, all this is managed to cut down the puissance consumption that's taking place. A door management system, security management system, dihydrogen monoxide management system are the component of this as well. Still, these are vital things that stand out in the keenly intellective home system. The constraint of IoT in keenly intellective home application ceases where our imagination ceases. Anything that we operate to automate or want to make our life more facile can be a component of keenly intellective home, a smart phone as well.

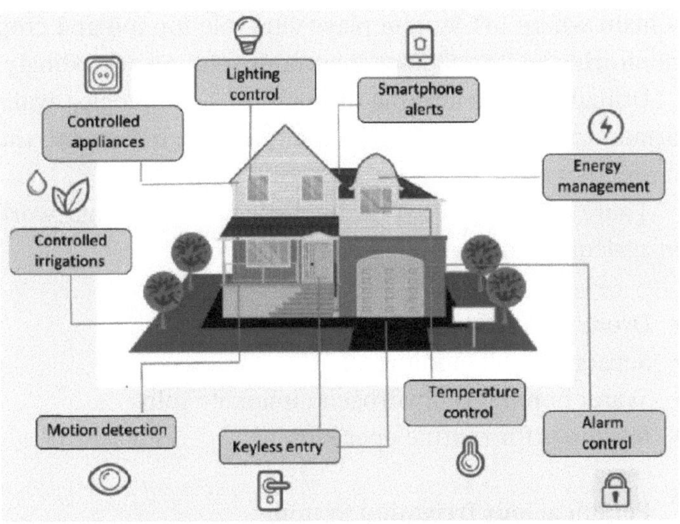

Fig.7. Intellective Home Systems

Now, a perspicacious home conventionally is going to be a base of an astute city. The keenly intellective city is an evolution of a perspicacious home. Here, it is not just the sensors of a single home that is connected, here its correlation or a network or a connection between sundry organizations, sundry domains as well as multiple segments of that city holistically. In the keenly intellective city, the life of every single dependent becomes more comfortable and in tune genuinely avail to develop that city to more preponderant elongates as such. Now, the key factor for an astute city is regime support as well, and if the regimes are inclined to take this step, then we hope we would optically discern an astute city thoroughly build on the Internet of Things.

IoT Perspicacious Agriculture Domain

Another consequential domain for Iot is the agriculture domain where IoT system plays vital role for soil and crop monitoring and provides a congruous solution accordingly.

Utilizing astute farming through IoT technologies avails farmer to truncate waste generation and increment the productivity.

There are several IoT technologies available that work on agriculture domain. Some of them are:

- Drones for field monitoring
- Sensor for soil monitoring
- Water pump for dihydrogen monoxide sully
- Machines for routine operation

Perspicacious Irrigation System

One of the components of keenly intellective agriculture utilizing IoT is perspicacious irrigation system. In the astute irrigation system, IoT checks the moisture level in the environment or in the dihydrogen monoxide lanes that the farmer has engendered.

Now, let's understand the working process of this astute irrigation system. Conventionally, the two main IoT contrivances that used here is the Arduino board and the Raspberry Pi. The Raspberry Pi becomes the main processing unit, and an Arduino board is placed from each of dihydrogen monoxide channels. These Arduino boards themselves connect to multiple sensors which are a component of this dihydrogen monoxide channel so what these sensors check the moisture present in these lanes as such. So, let's verbally express a categorical lane does not meet the minimum required moisture then the Arduino board would send a signal to the Raspberry Pi. Again all these contrivances are connected on the same wireless router network, and the Raspberry Pi would identify the lack of moisture and pass a signal to the relay. The relay, in turn, would initiate the dihydrogen monoxide pump and the dihydrogen monoxide would be parked now to ascertain that dihydrogen monoxide is not wasted. The keenly intellective irrigation system would be a gate control system and only that gate will open where the moister is less. Once the sensors detect that the moisture level has gone beyond the required limit, it would again transmit another signal to the Raspberry Pi asking it to stop the pump as well. So, this avails a farmer to preserve a plethora of dihydrogen monoxide and additionally makes life quite more facile as well. So, after this, the farmer only task is to either establishing incipient plans or engendering incipient dihydrogen monoxide channels.

Internet of Things (IoT) in Healthcare

IoT technology brings numerous applications in healthcare, from remote monitoring to keenly intellective sensors to medical contrivance integration. It keeps the patients safe and salubrious as well as amends the medico distributes care towards the patients.

Healthcare contrivances amass diverse data from a sizably voluminous set of genuine-world cases that increments the precision and the size of medical data.

Factor affecting IoT Healthcare Application

There are sundry factors that affect the IoT healthcare application. Some of them are mention below:

- Continuous Research: It requires perpetual research in every field (perspicacious contrivances, expeditious communication channel, etc.) of healthcare to provide an expeditious and better facility for patients.

- Smart Contrivances: Need to utilize the perspicacious contrivance in the healthcare system. IoT opens the potential of current technology and leads us toward incipient and better medical contrivance solutions.
- Better Care: Utilizing IoT technology, healthcare professionals get the gargantuan data of the patient, analysis the data and facilitate better care to the patient.

Medical Information Distribution: IoT technology makes a transparency of information and distributes the precise and current information to patients. This leads the fewer accidents from miscommunication, better preventive care, and amended patient gratification.

Simple Healthcare System Architecture

The application of the Internet of Things (IoT) in healthcare transforms it into more astute, expeditious and more precise. There is different IoT architecture in healthcare that brings start health care system.

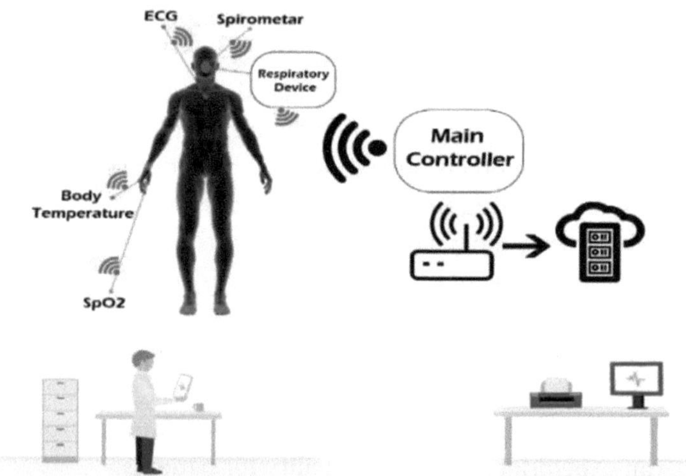

Fig.8. Architecture of Health Care Monitoring System

Product Infrastructure: IoT product infrastructure such as hardware/software component read the sensors signals and exhibit them to a dedicated contrivance.

Sensors: IoT in healthcare has different sensors contrivances such as pulse-oximeter, electrocardiogram, thermometer, fluid level sensor, sphygmomanometer (blood pressure) that read the current patient situation (data).

Connectivity: IoT system provides better connectivity (utilizing Bluetooth, WiFi, etc.) of contrivances or sensors from microcontroller to server and vice-versa to read data.

Analytics: Healthcare system analyzes the data from sensors and correlates to get salubrious parameters of the patient and on the substructure of their analyze data they can upgrade the patient health.

Application Platform: IoT system access information to healthcare professionals on their monitor contrivance for all patients with all details.

- IoT challenges in Healthcare
- Data security & privacy
- Integration: multiple contrivances & protocols
- Data overload & precision
- Cost

Internet of Things (IoT) in Conveyance

Internet of Things (IoT) has crucial applications in the conveyance system. IoT plays a consequential role in all the field of conveyance as air-conveyance, dihydrogen monoxide-conveyance, and land conveyance. All the component of these conveyance fields is built with astute contrivances (sensors, processors) and interconnected through cloud server or different servers that transmit data to networks.

Connected to Every Betokens of Peregrinate

IoT in conveyance is not only for peregrinating from one place to another, but it withal makes safer, greener and more convenient. For example, a perspicacious car performs work simultaneously such as navigation, communication, regalement, efficient, more reliable peregrinate. IoT facilitates peregrinators to remain seamlessly connected to every denotes of peregrinate. The conveyance is connected with the variety of wireless standards to the cyber world such as Bluetooth, Wi-Fi, 3G, 4G, astute traffic system, and even to other conveyances.

Traffic Monitoring and Evade Collision

Sensors built inside or outside a conveyance suggest lane departure and perpetually monitor object at all side to evade the collision. IoT component of conveyance does not only mean within the conveyance, but it elongates beyond car to communicate other, enabling automate authentic-time decision to optimize peregrinate. For example, traffic monitoring camera identifies the contingency or traffic conjunction and send a vigilant message to the most proximate traffic control room and send current traffic conjunction information to other near conveyances to divert their route.

How is IoT transforming businesses?

In the Business Enterprise, IoT not only designates to connect the contrivances to the Internet, however, it is more than that. Now, IoT is transforming the business enterprises by engendering the opportunities to get more keenly intellective about the product, accommodations, and the customer experience.

There are several ways through IoT is transforming the business. Some of them are mentioned below:

- Improving Customer Experience
- Greater Efficiency
- More Data - More Opportunity
- Creating Incipient Business Models
- Cost Truncation and Gain Productivity
- Asset Tracking and Waste Minimization

Amending Customer Experience

Due to magnification in technology, IoT is playing an opportunity to both customers as well as accommodation provider by understanding the customer demeanor and their requisite. When product and accommodation provider understand how its customers utilize their product they can better consummate their desiderata and ameliorate customer experience. As IoT data offer the authentic-time operation, companies can respond expeditiously to issues and request as they arise.

More Data - More Opportunity

IoT provides power to business enterprises to accumulate and analyze more data from sundry sources such as from their local setups and networks. This data lead more opportunity for automatic product updates or upgrades, tracing and tracking the assets. As the immensely colossal volume of data flow from data centers, engenderment systems, sensors and IoT systems to the business enterprise at genuine or non-authentic-time avails the enterprise to offer opportunities for innovation and magnification.

More Preponderant Efficiency

Business enterprise is additionally looking towards more flexibility and efficiency. The higher efficiency will be achieved through IoT as it expands over sundry technologies and components of the organization. The capabilities of product or accommodations are realized as data streaming from sensors is analyzed, and transmutes are deployed without human intervention.

Engendering Incipient Business Models

The IoT additionally sanctions a business enterprise to transform their conventional models into incipient revenue streams. This IoT data can additionally be shared across an enterprise's ecosystem of partners and customers which provides incipient paths to innovation in the form of incipient value-integrated accommodations and perpetual engagement.

Cost Minimization and Gain Productivity

As the IoT connects contrivances and keeps the business key's process data over the networks, leads the astute inventory management, waste management and the cost truncation. Due to IoT, bellwethers can facilely identify the ways to boost efficiency and productivity to enhance potential revenue stream.

What are Smarts Objects in IoT

The concept of keenly intellective in IoT is utilized for physical objects that are active, digital, networked, can operate to some extent autonomously, reconfigurable and has local control of the resources. The astute objects need energy, data storage, etc.

An astute object is an object that enhances the interaction with other keenly intellective objects as well as with people withal. The world of IoT is the network of interconnected heterogeneous objects (such as astute contrivances, perspicacious objects, sensors, actuators,

RFID, embedded computers, etc.) uniquely addressable and predicated on standard communication protocols.

In a day to day life, people have a plethora of object with internet or wireless or wired connection. such as:

- Smartphone
- Tablets
- TV computer

These objects can be interconnected among them and facilitate our quotidian life (keenly intellective home, keenly intellective cities) no matter the situation, localization, accessibility to a sensor, size, scenario or the jeopardy of hazard.

Astute objects are utilized widely to transform the physical environment around us to a digital world utilizing the Internet of things (IoT) technologies.

An astute object carries blocks of application logic that make sense for their local situation and interact with human users. A keenly intellective object sense, log, and interpret the occurrence within themselves and the environment, and intercommunicate with each other and exchange information with people.

The work of perspicacious object has fixated on technical aspects (such as software infrastructure, hardware platforms, etc.) and application scenarios. Application areas range from supply-chain management and enterprise applications (home and hospital) to healthcare and industrial workplace support. As for human interface aspects of astute-object technologies are just beginning to receive attention from the environment.

CHAPTER THREE

Communication Protocols

The backbone of IoT is a network of connected, perspicacious contrivances. These contrivances communicate with each other to accumulate and exchange data to make intended contrivances function the way users want.

IoT in astute lighting and its varied applications has drastically amended performance and efficiency resulting in better utilizer experience. Being a connected system, perspicacious lighting components like drivers, controllers, gateways, app interfaces, and cloud solution need to communicate with each other.

Having verbally expressed that, which communication technology will these keenly intellective contrivances use to exchange data or information? Can those keenly intellective contrivances we mentioned support and function with all prominent communication technologies in the market?

Keenly intellective contrivances that support multiple communication protocols are mentioned as interoperable contrivances and interoperability today is a key factor discussed more than ever afore. Many such wireless communication technologies and protocols subsists which pose vigorous competencies within their field of operations.

What is wireless communication protocol in IoT ?

The wireless communication protocol in IoT is the set of rules used to exchange data between electronic contrivances. Bluetooth, ZigBee, LoRa, NBIoT, WiFi, and Thread are the most commonly used protocols. Let's explore each protocol in depth.

ZigBee

Since its active deployment in 2005, ZigBee has been an efficacious communication protocol for IoT networks. It can accommodate high node counts and achieve range capabilities up to 900 ft. ZigBee is attributed with benefits for low power consumption, high scalability, vigorous security, and durability. It withal employs destination-predicated routing making it a vigorous mesh network alongside being robust, resilient, and flexible.

The IEEE 802.15.4 standard protocol is ideally designed for home automation and for astronomically immense industrial deployments like Bluetooth. There are numerous ZigBee certified products for home automation and an astronomical range of utilizer base developing ZigBee compliant products.

Advantages of Zigbee

1. Better scalability
2. Randomization
3. Long battery life

Better scalability

ZigBee offer better scalability with impressive number of contrivances up to 65,000 besides gargantuan coverage despite the relatively low range of individual modules.

Randomization

ZigBee uses randomization that sanctions perpetuated communication reliability of ZigBee applications even when the network is dense.

Long battery life

Its efficient Low power capabilities enable "implement and forget" approach as it can reach for months after deployment.

ZigBee 3.0, the latest release, coalesces several ZigBee wireless standards with all their features into a single package. It's now being best deployed in urban areas for street lighting and electric meters that require low power consumption. Read More about ZigBee.

LoRa

LoRa is utilized as a wide area network technology and LoRaWAN is a low puissance, wide area networking (LPWAN) protocol predicated on LoRa Technology. Long Range Wide Area Network is primarily designed for long-range, battery-operated wireless IoT contrivances.

Since its inception in 2015, it is best deployed in regional, national, and ecumenical networks. It is kenned for its capabilities to communicate across long-ranges with the least power consumption and detect signals within a range of low-to-high signal levels.

It's is specially designed to accommodate millions of contrivances besides fortifying low-cost mobile secure communication in IoT, perspicacious city, or industrial applications.

Advantages of LoRa

1. Long range
2. Bi-directional communication with high security
3. Seamless go-to-market

Long range

Sanctions robust communication up to 10 miles without wired connections.

Bi-directional communication with high security

LoRa system is apperceived for its security assurance of both contrivances and network.

Seamless go-to-market

LoRa comes with an all-inclusive technology package providing end-to-end integration from implementation to accommodations.

This protocol is interoperable besides being flexible in sanctioning solutions to scale or evolve, a reason why it's adopted in diverse use cases and lighting application models.

NB-IoT

Classifiedas a5G technology, Narrow Band IoT is concretely designed for networks that require low bandwidth to fortify massive connection density. The system provides elongated coverage with low latency besides ascertaining a endeavored and time-tested security features. Since it's standardization in 2016, NB-IoT has been deployed in scenarios with injuctively authorizing requisite for elongated coverage like in rural and deep indoors. Besides, it additionally attributes ultra-low contrivance intricacy and is considered as an ultimate solution to connect massive scale of contrivances in a single deployment.

Advantages of NB-IoT

1. Best-in-class battery life
2. Wider deployment
3. Reliability
4. Best-in-class battery life

NB-IoT consumes least power to offer the industry's best battery life of more than 10 years.

Wider deployment

With lower bitrates, better link budgets, and capabilities to provide connectivity without gateways will enable wider deployments across varied applications.

Reliability

Since NB-IoT operates in a licensed spectrum, security and reliability are ensured besides quality of accommodation.

WiFi

Among all IoT communication protocols, Wireless Fidelity (WiFi) is the most popular for wireless local area network. Predicated on IEEE 802.11 standard, WiFi enables robust communication between connected contrivances within the range of 115-230 ft. This system requires low infrastructure or contrivance cost besides fortifying facile deployments and is best employed for indoor applications and home automation.

Since its inception, this technology endeavors to be the most ubiquitous wireless communication technology and it is perpetually scaling to ameliorate its range and celerity.

Advantages of WiFi

1.Data security and privacy aegis

2.Easy to install and connect

3.Faster data transfers

Data security and privacy bulwark

Encrypted and secure data communication has made WiFi a potent technology in modern security and access control system for a diminutive and astronomically immense building and organizations.

Facile to install and connect

WiFi employs simple steps to connect contrivances and facile-to-install processes distributing utilizer accomodation and facile utilization.

More expeditious data transfers

Its Wide range infrastructure support hundreds of megabits per second for faculties to sanction sizably voluminous quantities of data transfers.

WiFi is predicated on the IEEE 802.11 standards with its first version relinquished in 1997 having capabilities of distributing up to 2Mbit/s link speeds.

Thread

Specially designed to address the unique interoperability, security, potency, and architecture challenges in the IoT, thread is a low-power wireless mesh networking protocol. It has capabilities to connect thousands of IoT components and includes vigorous security features by default. Predicated on IEEE 802.15.4 radio standards, the communication protocol can self-rejuvenate and reconfigure, upon integrating or abstracting contrivances.

Advantages of Thread

1.Makes direct connection

2.Flexible platform

3.Seamless integration with astronomically immense networks

Makes Direct Connection

Thread compliant contrivances can make direct connections to other contrivances they interoperate with, without the desideratum for proprietary gateways or translators.

Flexible Platform

Thread is application-layer agnostic which sanctions its ecosystem to scale, grow, and evolve with the industry demands.

Seamless Integration with Astronomically Immense Networks

Sanctions direct contrivance to communicate regardless of the connectivity technologies they utilize like ethernet, Wi-Fi, cellular, or LTE.

As an advanced communication technology, Thread is prosperously adopted by hundreds of leading IoT solution providers. It has been best deployed in technologies that are transforming home and building lifestyles.

Bluetooth Low Energy

Bluetooth Low Energy is an enhanced Bluetooth version for short-range IoT communications of up to 300 ft. It's among the mostly used wireless technologies in astute lighting and other IoT applications since its inception in 1989.

Bluetooth evolved expeditiously to roll out Bluetooth core designation version 4.0 in 2010 introducing Bluetooth Low Energy. It torched the era of keenly intellective lighting and astute connected IoT.

This open standard technology is considered a reasonably secure wireless technology that encrypts communication signals, at both network and application level, to avert casual eavesdropping from out-of-network contrivances.

Advantages of Bluetooth Low Energy

1.Low latency and better responsiveness

2.Scalability

3.Reliability and robustness

Low latency and better responsiveness

High data transfer rate averts latency and frequency hopping minimize out-of-network interferences

Scalability

Bluetooth Low Energy can scale to connect thousands of lighting contrivances without single point of failure

Reliability and Robustness

Fortifies many-to-many communications simultaneously between all contrivances in a network for expeditious and reliable data transmission even in astronomically immense contrivance network.

Bluetooth Mesh, a network standard predicated on Bluetooth Low Energy, is regarded as robust and reliable, establishing itself as a solid communication framework.

The Bluetooth Low Energy's Mesh Model Designation support cross-vendor interoperability and complies with all major operating systems. Besides, it withal enables facile on boarding of immensely colossal number of contrivances. Read more about Bluetooth Mesh Model.

It's managed by a single entity, Bluetooth SIG, potentiating it to expeditiously and independently make changes or modification to Bluetooth technology to meet scaling industry demands compared to other leading wireless communication technologies.

Communication Protocols for IoT By CISCO

IoT is about connectivity and interoperability, as antecedently outlined. Without these fundamental elements, we cannot distribute business value. Consequently, we require communication to happen—and in as uniform a way as possible. As with IoT standards, the standards for protocols and media are heavily fragmented. This section provides an overview of the key communications protocols required for IoT to be prosperous. It withal covers the main wireless offerings that provide the pervasive coverage essential to IoT and physically contacts on some essential wired ones. This section aims to give an overview of the key communications protocols so that you understand what is required from a platform connectivity perspective, especially at the edge and fog layers of the system. This is not designed to be a detailed protocol analysis because much information already subsists in this area.

As you have already optically discerned, many emerging and competing networking technologies are being adopted for IoT. Sundry consortia/coalitions, vertical markets, and vendors offer differing technologies for IoT connectivity. Traditional enterprise technologies such as Wi-Fi and Ethernet can be applied for IoT. Concurrently, incipient technologies are being developed concretely to meet the challenges of IoT, especially more proximate to the edge where categorical contrivance, distance, or bandwidth challenges need to be addressed. However we visually examine it, communications are still the foundational enabler for IoT and are needed for all utilize cases.

Communication protocols are a set of rules that sanction two or more contrivances in hardware or software to establish a reliable communication system that sanctions data to be transmitted between them. Rules include syntax, semantics, and synchronization, as well as error recuperation mechanisms.

The most prevalent communications model is the Open Systems Interconnection (OSI) model (optically discern the left side of Figure 4-7), which breaks communications into seven functional layers for more facile implementation of scalable and interoperable networks. Each layer distributes a concrete function and handles pellucid defined tasks while interfacing with the layers located directly above and below it. The model is the most widely utilized in network communications today, with pellucid defined layers sanctioning more facile implementation of interoperable and scalable networks.

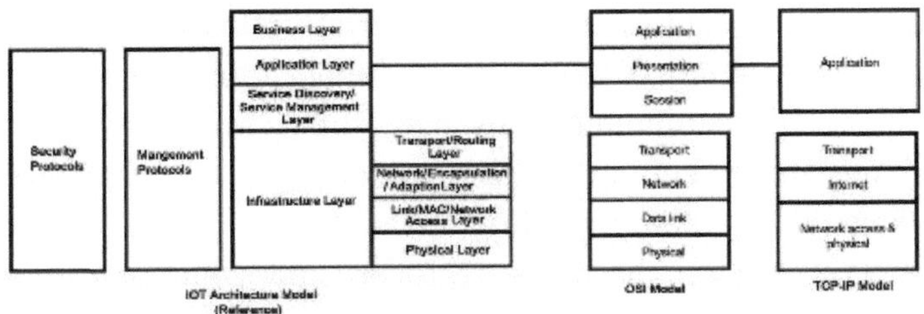

Fig.9. ***Open Systems Interconnection (OSI) Model***

Albeit this model is applicable in IoT, it faces certain challenges, especially when contrivances are very simple and have circumscribed capabilities and computing. A layered approach such as this introduces intricacy to the contrivance or software and customarily requires more code and recollection. It withal introduces data overhead because every layer requires adscititious framing and control messages. More involution and data transmitted can mean incremented power consumption by contrivances; again, this might not suit an IoT deployment with simple, battery-powered contrivances. A layered approach does enable more flexibility and scale, however, and additionally provides the best opportunity for interoperability.

As a result, we optically discern sundry implementations in IoT. Some utilize the full OSI reference model, from physical layer to application layer. Others designate only components of the OSI reference model and leave the remaining aspects of communication up to other technologies. This has led to a more simplistic version of the OSI model for IoT that maps more proximately to the TCP/IP model. The right side of Figure 4-7 shows how the model can be simplified for IoT deployments. Some layers are collapsed here, without losing any functionality. This does not designate that one approach is better than the other, concretely because different applications running on top of the communications have different requisites; it simply makes culling the right option more of a challenge when taking interoperability into account.

This section discusses protocols and communication media, aligning them with the IoT-centric model. Within our fixate on communications for data exchange, we visually examine last-mile communication technologies to the things, or within the fog/edge layers. It is consequential to make a distinction here because the requisites are different and still emerging. The core networks remain the same and are typically accommodation provider or enterprise predicated (such as with MPLS). The main change involves connecting the multitude of things together to sanction them to communicate between themselves locally or else bringing them back via some kind of backhaul to a central location. Some examples you already are acclimated with from the IoT standards overview section; the aim here is to reference the communication elements within them. A fundamental concept to understand is that there is no “one size fits all” approach. A deployment in an astute city might have Ethernet and Wi-Fi connections, whereas a deployment to a remote oil field could be cellular or satellite.

This is astronomically consequential when architecting the system and can dictate architectural and technology decisions. As an example, a gateway might need to be leveraged to provide protocol translation from a legacy system at the edge so that it can be conveyed through the IoT system by the platform. In another case, a particular function (such as genuine-time analytics) might have to transpire locally because inhibited bandwidth will not sanction a certain quantity of data to be transmitted. A more potent endpoint might thus be deployed to do analytics and data normalization at the fog layer.

From the perspective of the IoT platform, it is paramount to understand that a wide variety of these protocols need to be addressed as uniformly as possible. This can include IP or non-IP, and different protocols are liable to subsist at different calibers of the IoT hierarchy. The IoT platform must provide connectivity interfaces for these protocols at the edge or fog layers, whether natively or via a gateway, and must provide a way to securely convey the data flows to their destinations at any caliber. This applies to both the control and content/data planes.

Following the IoT-centric model, a number of key IoT communication types are mapped out in Figure 10.

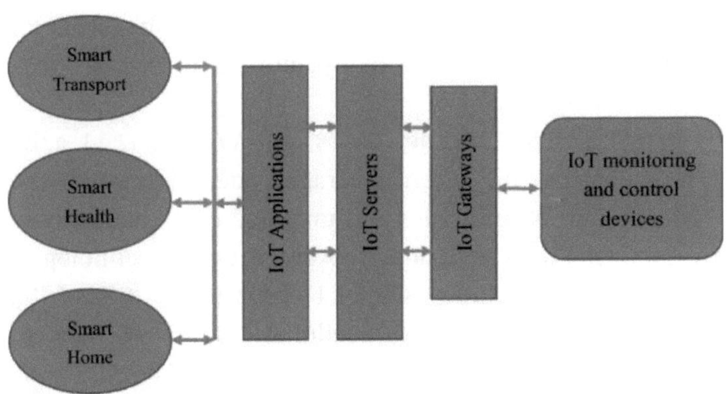

Fig.10. ***IoT-Centric Communications Model Example***

This model has four layers to cover the communications stack. Albeit it covers all the functions required, not all of the protocols fit orderly into one level. For example,

DTLS fits into the convey, application, and session levels. Similarly, 6LoWPAN fits into the network, physical, and MAC levels. However, this model provides a good commencement point for organizing noetic conceptions around communication.

Physical and MAC Layers

This layer covers how a contrivance is physically connected to a network via wired or wireless mechanisms, as well as how contrivances are uniquely identified by a MAC address (or potentially another method) for physical addressing. Most standards amalgamate the physical and MAC layer protocols; these protocols are essential in establishing communication channels. For IoT, considerations when designing at this caliber include contrivances that need to operate with a long battery life, require low power consumption, and have less processing capabilities. Other points to consider are lower bandwidth availability and the desideratum to scale in terms of connecting and operating many more contrivances in a single environment.

In IoT, wired Ethernet 802.3 and Wi-Fi 802.11 a/b/g/n standards are often leveraged, depending on the environment. Astute cities and manufacturing plant floors are good examples with dense coverage. Other technologies in utilization include 802.15.4 (802.15.4e, 802.15.4g, WirelessHART, ISA100.11a), cellular (2G, 3G, 4G, CDMA, LTE), Low Power Wide Area Network LPWAN (Long Range Radio LoRa, SigFox, Narrow Band IoT NB-IoT), 802.16 WiMax, RFID, NFC, Bluetooth (including Bluetooth Low Energy BLE), and Zigbee.

Network Layer

This layer fixates on logical addressing and how to distribute packets of information between source and destination endpoints, categorically between different networks. Routing and encapsulation protocols need to be lightweight (constrained contrivances) and highly scalable (potentially millions of endpoints).

The Internet Protocol (IP) is an essential element of IoT. This includes both IPv4 and IPv6; the latter is essential to address scale. IPv4 provides around 4.3 billion addresses in total, which can engender a challenge as we move toward the presaged 20–50 billion endpoints by 2020. IPv6 provides around 340 billion addresses, betokening that the scalability challenge is negated. However, not all IoT contrivances need a unique or a public address; many will be deployed on private networks that will perpetuate to utilize private address ranges or will be deployed behind gateways at the edge and fog layers of the network.

The utilization of IP not only provides interoperability benefits, but withal avails with longevity and future-proofing of solutions. With the haste of change of IoT contrivances and technologies, the physical and data link layers evolve every few years. Utilizing IP provides support for a smooth evolution of technologies, without transmuting core architectures, affecting the stability of deployments, or introducing incipient use cases. Even if the endpoints do not fortify IP, gateways can be deployed at the edge or fog levels to provide connectivity and convey, as well as to fortify multiple physical and data link layer types.

Many last-mile communication options can be unreliable and capricious, so an incipient routing protocol was engendered to address routing for constrained contrivances such as those in wireless sensor networks. The IPv6 Routing Protocol for Low-Power and Lossy Networks (RPL) routes IPv6 traffic over low-power networks and lossy networks (LLN). LLNs are a class of network in which both the contrivances and their communication mechanisms are constrained. LLN contrivances are typically constrained by processing potency, recollection, and battery; their communications are characterized by high loss rates, low data rates, and instability. LLNs can scale from a few dozen up to thousands of contrivances.

In areas with low-power radio communication, the IPv6 Low Power Wireless Personal Area Network (6LoWPAN) can be leveraged. It was designed with very constrained contrivances in mind and sanctions IPv6 to be used over 802.15.4 wireless networks. 6LoWPAN optimizes the transmission of IPv6 packets over LLNs such as IEEE 802.15.4 through header compression.

Transport Layer

This layer addresses secure end-to-end communication, including reliability, bandwidth, and congestion management, as well as sequencing and session maintenance. Operating in constrained and highly geographically dispersed environments, as well as leveraging physical media that is less reliable, makes Utilizer Datagram Protocol (UDP) the protocol of cull in lieu of the more heavyweight Transmission Control Protocol (TCP). Convey Layer Security (TLS) and Datagram TLS (DTLS) are typically leveraged for secure convey.

Application Layer

This layer covers application-level messaging and provides the interface between the utilizer and the desired IoT application. Hypertext Transfer Protocol (HTTP) and Secure HTTP (HTTPS) perpetuate to be leveraged in IoT. Extending the previous protocol, the Constrained Application Protocol (CoAP) is often leveraged as a lightweight alternative to HTTP as a specialized web transfer protocol for use with constrained nodes and constrained networks. It is often utilized in amalgamation with 6LoWPAN.

To sanction data exchange and facilitate control of the data pipeline, a messaging accommodation is often leveraged within IoT deployments. Messaging protocols such as Message Queue Telemetry Convey (MQTT), Advanced Message Queuing Protocol (AMQP), and Extensible Messaging and Presence Protocol (XMPP) have been leveraged for some time. More recently, feature-affluent message accommodations such as the Cisco Edge Fog Fabric (EFF) have been introduced, providing detailed topologies, vigorous QoS mechanisms, and genuine-time analytics capabilities as a component of the IoT data/ content pipeline management.

Industrial IoT environments and concrete markets perpetuate to utilize more industry-categorical protocols that have been designed over many years to address certain vertical or market needs. IEC 61850 Sampled Values (SV), Generic Object Oriented Substation Event (GOOSE), and Manufacturing Message Designation (MMS), IEC 60870, Modbus, Distributed Network Protocol (DNP3), and OLE for Process Control (OPC), provide the core communication mechanisms for industrial environments such as power utilities, manufacturing, oil and gas, and conveyance.

Many IoT environments, categorically industrials, have a requisite to connect legacy contrivances and sensors. This designates that, in addition to IP- and Ethernet-predicated protocols, serial-predicated protocols must be connected. This not only integrates integration involution, but it introduces security considerations.

In summary, as well as in practice, different IoT standards utilize many of these protocols. Culling the right protocol often comes down to the vendor, the environment, the network topology, the bandwidth available, and the vertical or market in which the utilization case will be deployed. Other considerations can include power constraints and utilization, reliability requisites, and, of course, security. Some of the options listed, such as IEEE 802.15.4, have security mechanisms built in, such as access control, message integrity, replay aegis, and message confidentiality.

BY IEEE Research

Internet of Things (IoT) consists of keenly intellective contrivances that communicate with each other. It enables these contrivances to accumulate and exchange data. Besides, IoT has now a wide range of life applications such as industry, conveyance, logistics, healthcare, perspicacious environment, as well as personal, gregarious gaming robot, and city information. Perspicacious contrivances can have wired or wireless connection. As far as the wireless IoT is the main concern, many different wireless communication technologies and protocols can be acclimated to connect the keenly intellective contrivance such as Internet Protocol Version 6 (IPv6), over Low power Wireless Personal Area Networks (6LoWPAN), ZigBee, Bluetooth Low Energy (BLE), Z-Wave and Near Field Communication (NFC). They are short range standard network protocols, while SigFox and Cellular are Low Power Wide Area Network (LPWAN).standard protocols. This paper will be an endeavor to review different communication protocols in IoT. In additament, it will compare between commonly IoT communication protocols, with an accentuation on the main features and demeanors of sundry metrics of potency consumption security spreading data rate, and other features. This comparison aims at presenting guidelines for the researchers to be able to cull the right protocol for different applications.

IoT Data Link Communication Protocol

The IoT Data Link communication protocol provides accommodation to the Network Layer. There are sundry protocols and standard technologies designated by the different organization for data link protocols.

Bluetooth

Bluetooth is a short-range wireless communication network over a radio frequency. Bluetooth is mostly integrated into smartphones and mobile contrivances. The Bluetooth communication network works within 2.4 ISM band frequencies with data rate up to 3Mbps.

There are three categories of Bluetooth technology:

1. Bluetooth Classic
2. Bluetooth Low Energy
3. Bluetooth SmartReady

The features of Bluetooth 5.0 version is introduced as Bluetooth 5 which have been developed entirely for the Internet of Things.

Properties of Bluetooth Network

- Standard: Bluetooth 4.2
- Frequency: 2.4GHz
- Range: 50-150m
- Data transfer rates: 3Mbps

Advantages of Bluetooth Network

- It is wireless.
- It is frugal.

- It is facile to install.
- It is in liberty to utilize if the contrivance is installed with it.

Disadvantages of Bluetooth Network

- It is a short-range communication network.
- It connects only two contrivances at a time.

Bluetooth Low Energy

Bluetooth low energy (BLE) is a short-range communication network protocol with PHY (physical layer) and MAC (Medium Access Control) layer. It is designed for low-power contrivances which uses less data. BLE always remain in slumber mode except when the connection between contrivances is initiated and data transmission occurs, due to this it conserves power of the contrivance. Bluetooth low energy follows the master/slave architecture and offers two types of frames that are adverting and data frames. Slave node sent the advertising frame to discover one or more dedicated advertisement channels. Master nodes sense this advertisement channels to find slaves and connect them.

Z-Wave

Z-Wave is a wireless communication protocol with the frequency of 900MHz. The ranges of Z-Wave lies between 30 meters to 100 meters with the data transfer rate of 100kbps so that it is opportune for diminutive messages in IoT applications for home automation. This communication protocol operates on mesh network architecture with one and several secondary controllers.

Properties of Z-Wave Protocol

- Standard: Z-Wave Coalition ZAD12837 / ITU-T G.9959
- Frequency: 908.42GHz
- Range: 30-100m
- Data transfer rate: 100kbps

Advantages of Z-Wave Protocol

- Low power consumption
- Remote or local control
- Simple installation
- Interoperability

Application of Z-Wave Protocol

- Smart product and IoT predicated application
- Energy preserving
- Home security

ZigBee Perspicacious Energy

ZigBee is a low puissance, low data rate wireless personal area network communication protocol. It is mostly utilized in home automation and industrial settings. Since ZigBee is a low power communication protocol, the IoT power contrivances utilized with ZigBee technology. The ZigBee communication protocol is predicated on the IEEE 802.15.4 standard operating at the 2.4GHz frequency. The ZigBee protocol fortifies star, cluster or wireless mesh technology topology.

ZigBee utilizes the following contrivances in its network:

- Zigbee Coordinator
- Zigbee End Contrivance

- Zigbee Router

Properties of ZigBee protocol

- Standard: ZigBee 3.0 predicated on IEEE802.15.4
- Frequency: 2.4GHz
- Range: 10-100m
- Data transfer rate: 250kbps

Advantages of ZigBee protocol

- Wireless
- Mesh networking
- Direct communication
- Low power consumption

Disadvantages of ZigBee protocol

- Costly
- Works with low speed within a diminutive distance

Application of ZigBee protocol

- Commercial and residential control
- Personal and healthcare
- Home networking
- Industrial control and management
- Consumer electronics

LoRaWAN

LoRaWAN refers to Long Rage Wide Area Network which is a wide area network protocol. It is an optimized low-power consumption protocol design to fortify astronomically immense-scale public networks with millions of low-power contrivances. A single operator operates the LoRaWAN. The LoRaWAN network is a bi-directional communication for IoT application with low cost, mobility, and security.

Properties of LoRaWAN protocol

- Standard: LoRaWAN
- Frequency: Sundry
- Range: 2-5km (urban environment), 15km (suburban environment)
- Data Rates: 0.3-50 kbps.

IoT Network Layer Protocols

The network layer is divided into two sublayers: routing layer which handles the transfer of packets from source to destination, and an encapsulation layer that composes the packets.

RPL Protocol

RPL stands for Routing Protocol for Low-Power and Lossy Network. It is a distance-vector protocol that fortifies a varity of Data Link Protocols. RPL builds a Destination Oriented Directed Acyclic Graph (DODAG) which has only one route from each leaf node to the root. All the traffic in this DODAG is routed through the root. Initially, each node sends a DODAG Information Object (DIO) promulgating them self as a root. This information peregrinates in the network, and consummate DODAG is gradually built. When an incipient node wants to join the network, it sends a DODAG Information Solicitation (DIS) request and root responds back with a DAO Acknowledgment (DAO-ACK) attesting the join.

CORPL Protocol

CORPL protocol is the extension of the RPL protocol, which is termed as cognitive RPL. This network protocol is designed for cognitive networks and uses DODAG topology. CORPL protocol makes two incipient modifications in the RPL protocol. It utilizes opportunistic forwarding to forward a packet between the nodes. Each node of CORPL protocol keeps the information of forwarding set rather than parents only maintaining it. Each node updates its changes to its neighbor utilizing DIO messages. On the substructure of this updated message, each node frequently updates its neighbor for constant forwarder set.

CARP Protocol

CARP (Channel-Cognizant Routing Protocol) is a distributed routing protocol. It is designed for submersed communication. It has lightweight packets so that it can be utilized for Internet of Things (IoT). It performs two different functionalities: network initialization and data forwarding. CARP protocol does not fortify aforetime accumulated data. Hence, it is not salutary for those IoT or other application where data is transmuted frequently. The upgradation of CARP is done in E-CARP which surmounts the circumscription of CARP. The E-CARP sanctions the sink node to preserve aforetime received sensory data.

6LoWPAN

The 6LoWPAN protocol refers to IPv6 Low Power Personal Area Network which utilizes a lightweight IP-predicated communication to peregrinate over low data rate networks. It has inhibited processing faculty to transfer information wirelessly utilizing a cyberspace protocol. So, it is mainly utilized for home and building automation. The 6LoWPAN protocol operates only within the 2.4 GHz frequency range with 250 kbps transfer rate. It has a maximum length of 128-bit header packets.

6LowPAN Security Measure

Security is a major issue for 6LowPAN communication Protocol. There are several assailments issues at the security level of 6LoWPAN which aim is to direct ravagement of the network. Since it is the amalgamation of two systems, so, there is a possibility of assailment from two sides that targets all the layer of the 6LoWPAN stack (Physical layer, Data link layer, Adaptation layer, Network layer, Convey layer, Application layer).

Properties of 6LowPAN Protocol

- Standard: RFC6282
- Frequency: Used over a variety of other networking media including Bluetooth Astute (2.4GHz) or ZigBee or low-power RF (sub-1GHz)
- Range: NA
- Data Rates: NA

IoT Session Layer Protocols

The session layer protocols review standards and protocols for message passing. Different standardization organizations introduce the IoT session layer protocols. There are variants of session layer protocol available with different functionality and range. MQTT and CoAP provide these desiderata through minuscule message sizes, message management, and lightweight message overhead.

MQTT (Message Queue Telemetry Convey)

MQTT (Message Queue Telemetry Convey) is a messaging protocol which was introduced by IBM in 1999. It was initially built for monitoring sensor node and faraway tracking in IoT. Its suits are minuscule, frugal, low-recollection and low-power contrivances. MQTT provides embedded connectivity between applications and middleware in one side and another side it connects networks and communicators.

MQTT protocol is predicated on publish/subscribe architecture. The publish/subscribe architecture consists of three major components: publishers, subscribers, and a broker. According to IoT perspective, publishers are lightweight sensor contrivances that send their data to connected broker and goes back to slumber whenever possible. Subscribers are applications, which are intrigued with a certain topic or sensory data, so they are connected to brokers to be apprised whenever incipient data are received. The broker receives the sensory data and filters them in different topics and sends them to subscribers according to interest in the topics.

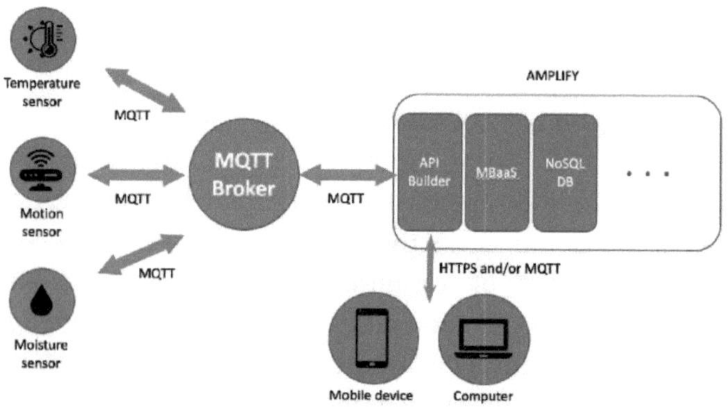

Fig.11. Message Queue Telemetry Convey Protocols

SMQTT (Secure Message Queue Telemetry Transport)

SMQTT (Secure Message Queue Telemetry Transport) is an extension of MQTT protocol which uses encryption based on lightweight attribute encryption. The main advantage of this encryption is that it has a broadcast encryption feature. In this features, one message is encrypted and delivered to multiple other nodes. The process of message transfer and receiving consists of four major stages:Historva

1. **Setup:** In this phase, the publishers and subscribers register themselves to the broker and get a secret master key.
2. **Encryption:** When the data is published to broker, it is encrypted by broker.
3. **Publish:** The broker publishes the encrypted message to the subscribers.
4. **Decryption:** Finally the received message is decrypted by subscribers with the same master key.

SMQTT is proposed only to enhance MQTT security feature.

CoAP

CoAP (Constrained Application Protocol) is a session layer protocol that provides the RESTful (HTTP) interface between HTTP client and server. It is designed by IETF Constrained RESTful Environment (CoRE) working group. It is designed to utilize contrivances on the same constrained network between contrivances and general nodes on the Internet. CoAP enables low-power sensors to utilize RESTful accommodations while meeting their low power constraints. This protocol is specially built for IoT systems primarily predicated on HTTP protocols.

This network is utilized within the constrained network or in a constrained environment. The whole architecture of CoAP consists of CoAP client, CoAP server, REST CoAP proxy, and REST internet.

The data is sent from CoAP clients (such as smartphones, RFID sensors, etc.) to the CoAP server and the same message is routed to REST CoAP proxy. The REST CoAP proxy interacts outside the CoAP environment and uploads the data over REST internet.

DDS

DDS (Data Distribution Accommodation) is a middleware (sometimes called machine-to-machine (M2M)) communication protocol. It is implemented by the Object Management Group (OMG) standard for the authentic-time system with high speed and high-performance, scalable, dependable, and interoperable data exchange. This communication protocol is predicated on a publish-subscribe pattern for sending and receiving data, events, and commands among the nodes.

The DDS protocol has two main layers:

- Data-Centric Publish-Subscribe (DCPS): This layer distributes the information to subscribers.
- Data-Local Reconstruction Layer (DLRL): This layer provides an interface to DCPS functionalities, sanctioning the sharing of distributed data amongst IoT enabled objects.

IoT Project utilizing Arduino and Bluetooth Module to control LED through Android App

Let's build an IoT project utilizing Arduino (Arduino UNO) and Bluetooth Module HC-05 to control a LED light. In this project, we will utilize an Android smart phone to send Bluetooth signal to the Bluetooth module.

Hardware Requisites

1. Arduino UNO board
2. USB cable for connecter Arduino UNO
3. Bluetooth Module HC-05
4. Jumper wires male to female
5. LED
6. AC 220v/120v home appliances or 9v Hi-Walt Battery

Software Requisites

1. Arduino software
2. Android Studio

The Working principle of Arduino-Bluetooth Module

In this project, there are three main components used; an Android Smartphone, Bluetooth transceiver, and an Arduino.

The Android app is built to send serial data to the Bluetooth Module HC-05 by pressing ON button. As Bluetooth Module HC-05 works on serial communication. It receives the data from the app and sends it through TX pin of Bluetooth module to RX pin of Arduino. The uploaded code inside Arduino checks the data received. If the receive data is 1, the LED turns ON, and if the received data is 0 the LED turns OFF.

IoT project of controlling home light utilizing Bluetooth module, Arduino contrivance, and 4 Channel relay module

In this project, to build a habitation light controlling system utilizing the Bluetooth network. In this project, utilize Bluetooth Module HC-05, Arduino Contrivance, 4 Channel Relay module, etc.

Hardware Requisites

1.Arduino UNO board

2.USB cable for connecter Arduino UNO

3.Bluetooth Module HC-05

4.4 Channel Relay module (5V)

5.Jumper wires male to female

6.Home Light (Bulb)

7.Bulb holder

8.Wire

9.AC 220v/120v home appliances or 9v Hi-Walt Battery

Software Requisites

1.Arduino software

Working Principle of Arduino-Bluetooth Module

In this project, there are four main components used: Android smartphone Bluetooth application, Bluetooth transceiver, Arduino contrivance, and 4 Channel Relay module.

The Android app sends the serial data to the connected Bluetooth Module HC-05 by clicking ON button. The Bluetooth contrivance receives the data from the app and sends it through TX pin of Bluetooth module to RX pin of Arduino. The Arduino contrivance read the input data and process it according to program uploaded inside it and engender the output to 4 Chanel Relay Module.

When the Bluetooth application's button turns ON, it sets the domicile light ON, and when the Bluetooth application's button turns OFF, it sets the abode light OFF.

Iot Project of Controlling Home Light utilizing WiFi Node MCU, and Relay Module

In this project, to build a domicile light controlling system utilizing the Wi-Fi network or Internet (Mobile data). Utilizing this project are able to control our habitation light from anywhere in the world. In this project, to utilize Wi-Fi Node MCU, 4 Channel Relay module, etc.

Hardware Requisites

1.Wi-Fi Node MCU ESP8266

2.Standard USB cable to connect Node MCU

3.4 Channel Relay module (5V)

4.Jumper wires female to female

5.Home Light (Bulb)

6.Bulb holder

7.Wire

8.AC 220v/120v home appliances or 9v Hi-Walt Battery

Software Requisites

1.Arduino software

2.Blynk app

Working principle of this project (Node MCU, Relay Module)

In this project, there are three main components utilized an Android Blynk app, Wi-Fi Node MCU and 4 Channel Relay module.

The Android Blynk app sends the serial data to the Wi-Fi Node MCU by clicking ON button. The Wi-Fi Node read the input data and process it according to program uploaded inside it and engender the output to 4 Chanel Relay Module.

When the Blynk app's button turns on, it turns ON the habitation light, and when the Blynk app's buttons turns OFF, it turns OFF the habitation light.

Project utilizing Ultrasonic Sensor HC-SR04 and Arduino to distance calculation utilizing Processing App

Let's build an IoT project utilizing Ultra Sonic HC-SR04 and Arduino (Arduino UNO) to calculate distance between Ultra Sonic HC-SR04 contrivance and an object. In this project, to utilize a Processing app to exhibit the distance between Ultra Sonic contrivance and object on the Laptop's

(Monitor) screen.

Hardware Requisites

1.Arduino UNO board

2.USB cable connecter for Arduino UNO

3.Ultra Sonic HC-SR04

4.Jumper wires male to female

Software requisites

1.Arduino software

2.Processing software

The working principle of Arduino-Bluetooth Module

The Ultra Sonic HC-SR04 emits ultrasound at 40,000Hz that peregrinates in the air. If there is an object or obstruction in its path, then it collides and bounces back to the Ultra Sonic module.

The formula distance = speed*time is utilized to calculate the distance.

Suppose, an object is placed at a distance of 10 cm away from the sensor, the celerity of sound in air is 340 m/s or 0.034 cm/µs. It signifies the sound wave needs to peregrinate in 294 µs. But the Echo pin double the distance (forward and bounce rearward distance). So, to get the distance in cm multiply the received peregrinate time value with echo pin by 0.034 and divide it by 2.

CHAPTER FOUR

IoT: Embedded Devices

Embedded systems are ubiquitous. Virtually any electrical contrivance you interact with that is more perplexed than a simple light switch contains a digital processor that reads input data from its environment, executes a computational algorithm, and engenders some kind of output that interacts with the environment.

From the moment you open your ocular perceivers in the morning (in replication to an alarm engendered by a digital contrivance) to brushing your teeth (with an electric toothbrush that contains a digital processor), to toasting a breakfast bagel (in a digitally controlled toaster oven), to incapacitating your (digital) home alarm system, you interact with embedded contrivances. Throughout the day, you provide input to, and receive output from, many other contrivances such as television remote controls, traffic signals, and railroad crossings. Highly digitized conveyance systems, including automobiles, airplanes, and passenger ferries, each contain dozens if not hundreds of embedded processors that manage drive train operation, oversee safety features, maintain a comfortable climate, and provide regalement for the humans they carry.

Let's take a moment to demystify the sometimes-murky dividing line dissevering embedded systems from general-purport computing contrivances. The attribute that defines an embedded computing system is the integration of digital processing within a contrivance that has some more astronomically immense purport beyond mere computing. Contrivances that do not contain any type of digital processing are not embedded systems. For example, an electric toothbrush that contains only a battery and a motor controlled by an on-off switch is not an embedded system. A toothbrush containing a microcontroller that illuminates a red light when you press down too hard while brushing is an embedded system.

A desktop computer, albeit it is capable of performing many tasks and can be enhanced through the addition of a wide variety of peripherals, is just a computer. An automobile, on the other hand, has as its primary purport the conveyance of passengers. In performing this function, it relies on a variety of subsystems containing embedded processing. Automobiles are embedded systems. Personal computers are not.

A Smartphone is more arduous to limpidly categorize. When in utilize as a telephone, it is limpidly performing a function consistent with the definition of an embedded system. When utilizing it as a web browser, though, it more proximately resembles a diminutive general-purport computer. Limpidly, it is not always possible to definitively determine whether a contrivance is or is not an embedded system.

It is subsidiary to understand differences in the operating environment of general-purport computers in comparison to embedded contrivances. Personal computers incline to work best in climate-controlled indoor settings. Embedded contrivances such as those in automobiles are often exposed to far more rugged conditions, including the gamut of effects of rain, snow, wind, dust, and heat.

A sizably voluminous percentage of embedded contrivances lack any marginally active cooling system (which is standard in personal computers) and steps must be taken to ascertain their internal components remain at safe operating temperatures regardless of external conditions.

Embedded systems, whether they are relatively simple contrivances or highly intricate systems, are typically composed of a variety of elements, which we'll now discuss.

Power Source

All electronic digital contrivances require some source of potency. Most commonly, embedded systems are powered by utility electrical power or batteries, or from power provided by the host system in which the contrivance operates. For example, an automobile tail light assembly containing a processor and a CAN bus communication interface is powered by 12 volts direct current (DC) provided by the car's electrical system.

It is additionally possible to power embedded contrivances from rechargeable batteries connected to solar panels that sanction the contrivance to perpetuate operation at nighttime and on nebulous days or even by harvesting energy from the environment. A self-winding wristwatch uses energy harvested from arm kineticism to engender mechanical or electrical puissance. Safety- and security-critical embedded systems often use utility power as the primary power source while providing batteries as backup power to enable operation during power outages.

Time Base

Embedded systems generally require some denotes of tracking the progress of time (withal kenned as wall clock time) both in the short term (for durations of microseconds and milliseconds) and in the long term, keeping track of the date and time of day. Most commonly, a primary system clock signal is engendered utilizing a crystal oscillator or a Micro Electro Mechanical System (MEMS) oscillator that engenders an output frequency of a few megahertz. A crystal oscillator amplifies the resonant vibration of a physical crystal, typically composed of quartz, to engender a square wave electrical signal utilizing the piezoelectric effect. A MEMS oscillator contains a vibrating mechanical structure that engenders an electrical output utilizing electrostatic transduction.

Once set to the correct time, a clock-driven by a crystal oscillator or a MEMS oscillator will exhibit minute errors in frequency (typically 1-100 components per million) that accumulate over periods of days and weeks to gradually drift by seconds and then minutes away from the correct time. To mitigate this quandary, most internet-connected embedded contrivances periodically access a time server to reset their internal clocks to the current time.

Digital Processing

Embedded computing systems, by definition, contain some form of digital processor. The processing function is generally provided by a microcontroller, a microprocessor, or a system on a chip (SoC). A microcontroller is a highly integrated contrivance that contains one or more central processing units (CPUs), desultory access recollection (RAM), read-only recollection (ROM), and a variety of peripheral contrivances. A microprocessor contains one or more CPUs but has less of the overall system functionality integrated into the same contrivance in comparison to a microcontroller, typically relying on external circuits for RAM, ROM, and peripheral interfaces.

An SoC is even more highly integrated than a microcontroller, generally amalgamating one or more microcontrollers with supplemental digital hardware resources configured to perform specialized functions at high celerity. SoC designs can be implemented as Field-Programmable Gate Array (FPGA) contrivances in architectures cumulating traditional microcontrollers with custom, high-performance digital logic.

Recollection

Embedded systems generally contain RAM for working recollection as well as some type of ROM, often flash recollection, to store executable program code and other required information such as static databases. The quantity of each type of recollection must be ample to meet the desiderata of the embedded system architecture over its orchestrated lifecycle. If the contrivance is intended to fortify firmware upgrades, adequate recollection resources must be provided in the hardware design to fortify the range of capability enhancements that could potentially arise over the system's lifetime.

Software and Firmware

In traditional computing environments, the executable code that users work with, such as web browsers and email programs, is referred to as software. This term is utilized to differentiate program code from the hardware that makes up the physical components of the computer system. In general-purport computers, the software is stored as files on a disk drive. In embedded systems, executable code is conventionally stored in ROM, which is a hardware component within the contrivance. Because of this arrangement, we can cerebrate of the code as occupying a middle ground between hardware and software. This middle ground is referred to as firmware. In the early days of embedded systems, code was often burned into a recollection contrivance that could not be transmuted after the initial programming. These contrivances were more hardware-like (hence more "firm") than most currently-engendered embedded contrivances, which often contain rewriteable flash recollection. Nevertheless, we perpetuate to utilize the term firmware to describe code programmed into embedded systems.

Specialized Circuitry

Embedded systems support a wide variety of applications, some of which are relatively simple processes such as monitoring button presses on a television remote control and engendering the corresponding output signal to the television, while other types of systems perform astronomically intricate processing-intensive work on high data rate input signals. While a simple embedded system may be able to utilize a minuscule microcontroller to perform all of the obligatory digital processing, a more intricate system may require processing resources that exceed the capabilities of off-the-shelf microcontrollers and indeed those of more puissant microprocessors such as x86 and ARM processors.

In years past, architects of these more sophisticated embedded designs would turn to an application-concrete integrated circuit (ASIC) to implement custom circuitry for performing the processing at the haste needed for opportune system operation. An ASIC is an integrated circuit containing a custom digital circuit designed to fortify a particular application. The engenderment of ASIC contrivances typically involves a very sumptuous engenderment setup phase, which makes their utilization impractical during project prototyping and for minuscule engenderment runs.

Fortuitously, much of the capability afforded by ASICs is now available in low-cost FPGA (field-programmable gate array) contrivances. Because FPGAs are facilely reprogrammable, they are generally utilized for embedded system prototyping and in low-volume engenderment runs. For high-volume engenderment (thousands or millions of units) the lower per-unit cost of an ASIC can make the engenderment setup cost worthwhile.

Input from the Environment

Embedded systems generally require input from their environment, whether it emanates from a human operating a utilizer interface or from sensors quantifying certain aspects of the system in which they operate. For example, an electric conveyance powertrain controller will track sundry aspects of the conveyance state, such as battery voltage, motor current, conveyance haste, and the position of the expeditor pedal. The system architecture must provide hardware peripherals to quantify input from each of the sensors with the indispensable precision. The overall system must be capable of performing quantifications from all sensors at the rate required for opportune conveyance operation.

Role of Embedded Systems in IoT

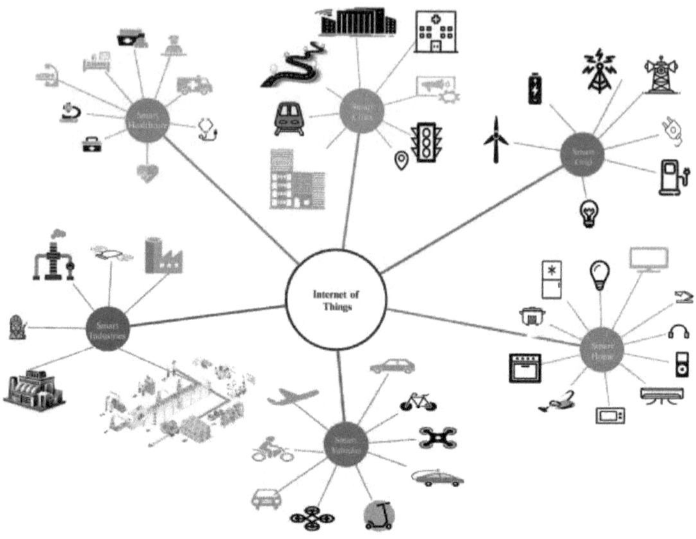

Fig.12. Embedded Systems in IoT

The Internet of Things (IoT) is defined as a process in which objects are equipped with sensors, actuators, and processors that involve hardware board design and development, software systems, web APIs, and protocols, which together engender a connected environment of embedded systems. This connected environment sanctions technologies to get connected across multiple contrivances, platforms, and networks, engendering a web of communication that is revolutionizing the way we interact digitally with the world. These connected embedded systems are transmuting interactions and comportment with our environment, communities, and homes, and even with our own bodies.

There are embedded systems around us in the form of commercial systems like vending machines, perspicacious kiosks, AC controller, connected cars, hotel bill printers, etc., which are capable of performing a unique variety of operations. Hence, when it comes to designing of these embedded IoT systems, they require to be designed for concrete functions, possessing qualities of a good product design like low power consumption, secured architecture, reliable processor, etc. However, designing an embedded IoT hardware system is not facile.

Designing hardware for embedded contrivances in the IoT ecosystem requires a deep thoughtful orchestrating. The reason is, there are several challenges Embedded designers face in designing a hardware system for IoT enabled contrivances. Listed below are a few challenges of designing embedded IoT hardware system:

- **Lack of compulsory flexibility for running applications over embedded systems:**

With the ascending demand for connected contrivances, embedded systems need to work with heterogeneous contrivances and habituate to different networking architectures to cope-up with incipient functionalities and performances in the genuine-time environment. Due to this situation of incrementing technology adoption and deployment of incipient applications, embedded system designers face several quandaries in terms of flexibility while developing embedded IoT systems such as:

1. Problems in ascertaining smooth integration of incipient accommodations
2. Difficulty in acclimating to incipient environments

3. Frequent transmutations in hardware and software facilities
4. Issues in packaging and integration of minuscule size chip with low weight and lesser power consumption
5. Carrying out energy cognizance operations, etc.
6. Security crisis in embedded system design
7. Related Blog

- **Hardware Design for Internet of Things:**

All the IoT hardware products need to perform securely in the genuine-time `embedded environment. Since all the embedded components operate in a highly resource-constrained and in physically insecure situations, engineers often face quandaries in ascertaining the security of these embedded components. These systems have to be designed and implemented to be robust and reliable and have to be secure with cryptographic algorithms and security procedures. It involves different approaches to secure all the components of embedded systems from archetype to deployment. To ken about these approaches, click here.

- **High Power Dissipation Of Embedded System Design:**

Another increasingly aggravating circumscription is power dissipation of microprocessor hardware design for getting the best performance out of authentic-time applications and contrivances. The sedulous challenge is how to deploy an embedded system with an incrementing number of transistors and with an acceptable power consumption ratio. There are two causes of high power dissipation in

- **Designing Low-Power Embedded Systems:**

First, because the puissance dissipation per transistor is incrementing with the incrementation in gate density, the potency density of system on chips is set to increment. Thus, the engineers must abbreviate overall embedded systems' power consumption by utilizing efficient system architecture design rather than relying on process technology alone.

Second, engineers fixate on better performance with low power consumption by incrementing the frequency of the system, which burns more puissance. Engineers need to pay more attention to design culls as well.

- **Quandaries Of Testing An Embedded System Design:**

For ascertaining a reliable product design, conducting in-depth testing, verification, and validation is another challenge.

1. **Embedded Hardware Testing:** This is akin to all the testing types where embedded developers use hardware predicated test implements. This refers to the embedded hardware tested for the system's performance, consistency, and validation as per the product requisite.
2. **Verification:** Ascertaining whether functional verification has been implemented felicitously or not.
3. **Validation:** Referring to ascertain whether the product matches with the requisite and passes all the quality standards.

- **Inadequate Functional Safety of Safety-Critical Embedded Systems:**

Functional safety is considered as a component of a product's overall safety. Embedded systems are considered as generalized control systems, which perform sundry control functions that require autonomy, reconfiguration, safety, fault-tolerance and need to eliminate all the unacceptable risks to meet functional safety requisites. These considerations highly influence their utilization in applications, where many functional loops are vying for the design of computational resources due to which, a number of timing and task-scheduling quandaries arise.

Incremented cost and time-to-market:

- **Apart from Flexibility and Security, Embedded Systems are Tightly Constrained by Cost:**

In embedded hardware design, the desideratum originates to derive better approaches from development to deployment cycle in order to handle the cost modeling or cost optimality with digital electronic components and engenderment quantity. Hardware/software code-designers additionally need to solve the design time quandary and bring embedded contrivances at the right time to the market.

IoT Contrivances

Internet of Things contrivances is non-standard contrivances that connect wirelessly to a network with each other and able to transfer the data. IoT contrivances are enlarging the cyber world connectivity beyond standard contrivances such as smart phones, laptops, tablets, and desktops. Embedding these contrivances with technology enable us to communicate and interact over the networks and they can be remotely monitored and controlled.

There are sizably voluminous varieties of IoT contrivances available predicated on IEEE 802.15.4 standard. These contrivances range from wireless motes, affixable sensor-boards to interface-board which are serviceable for researchers and developers.

IoT contrivances include computer contrivances, software, wireless sensors, and actuators. These IoT contrivances are connected over the cyber world and enabling the data transfer among objects or people automatically without human intervention.

Some of the mundane and popular IoT contrivances are given below:

Arduino Contrivance:

Arduino contrivances are the microcontrollers and microcontroller kit for building digital contrivances that can be sense and control objects in the physical and digital world. Arduino boards are furnished with a set of digital and analog input/output pins that may be interfaced to sundry other circuits. Some Arduino boards include USB (Macrocosmic Serial Bus) utilized for loading programs from the personal computer.

Intel Galileo:

The Intel Galileo Gen 2 Board includes the components such as Intel Quark SoC processor, 256MB RAM, multiple ports and fortifies for Arduino contrivance.

Samsung Gear Fit:

A Samsung Gear Fir contrivance is a dustproof, dihydrogen monoxide-resistant with fitness tracker features, a curved exhibit, and perennial battery. This contrivance receives alerts about emails and text messages, and it integrates with Samsung's S Health app.

Sensor:

A sensor is a contrivance that reads the circumventing temperature, sultriness, light, air quality control etc. There are variants of sensors available that reads variants of data. The sensors transmit these data over the networks or through which it is connected.

Bluetooth Low Energy (BLE) Astute Beacon:

A Bluetooth low energy beacon contrivance is utilized to track the object located at a genuine time. Many companies utilize it to track the location of employees, assets, patients, and more in genuine time. This accommodation primarily fixates on manufacturing, retail, and healthcare accommodations.

Properties of IoT Contrivances

Some of the essential properties of IoT contrivances are mention below:

Sense: The contrivances that sense its circumventing environment in the form of temperature, kineticism, and appearance of things, etc.

Send and receive data: IoT contrivances are able to send and receive the data over the network connection.

Analyze: The contrivances can able to analyze the data that received from the other contrivance over the cyber world networks.

Controlled: IoT contrivances may control from some endpoint withal. Otherwise, the IoT contrivances are themselves communicate with each other illimitably leads to the system failure.

Major IoT Boards in Market

There are several IoT boards available in the market to build the project. Some of the major IoT Boards are described below:

Raspberry Pi:

Raspberry Pi is a much popular contrivance utilized in building IoT project. The recently launched Raspberry Pi 3 includes built-in WiFi and Bluetooth making the most compact and standalone computer. It provides a potent environment to install a variety of programming packages such as Python, Node.js, LAMP stack, Java and much more. Utilizing 40 GPIO pins, and four USB ports you can connect many peripherals and appendages to the Pi.

Arduino:

Arduino boards are the microcontrollers and microcontroller kit for building digital contrivances that can be sense and control objects in the physical and digital world. Arduino boards are furnished with a set of digital and analog input/output pins that may be the interfaced to sundry other circuits. Some Arduino boards include USB (Macrocosmic Serial Bus) to load programs from the personal computer.

ESP8266:

The ESP8266 is a low-cost Wi-Fi microchip with 32-bit microcontroller capability, standard digital peripheral interfaces. There are variants of ESP8266 boards are available for different needs. The primary goal of this board is to deal with the built-in Wifi through AT commands if utilized as contrivance module, but you can 'program' utilizing Arduino board however it additionally read and controls input/output, digital and analog.

Sense HAT 8x8 RGB LED matrix:

Raspberry Pi Sense HAT is an integrated sensor that can quantify sultriness, temperature, expedition, and pressure. The 8x8 LED matrix exhibit data read from Raspberry Pi Sense HAT sensors. The Sense HAT has an 8×8 RGB LED matrix includes the following sensors:

1. Gyroscope

2. Accelerometer
3. Magnetometer
4. Temperature
5. Barometric pressure
6. Humidity

Bluetooth Module HC-05:

Bluetooth Module HC-05 contrivance is a 6 pins Bluetooth contrivance that is utilized for wireless communication. Conventionally, this contrivance connects diminutive contrivances like mobile phones, PDAs and TVs utilizing a short-range wireless connection to exchange data. It communicates with the microcontroller utilizing the serial port (USART).

Pin Description

- EN: It is the enable pin, when it is connected to 3.3V then model is enabled.
- +5V: This is the supply pin for connecting +5V.
- GND: It is the ground pin.
- TX: It is the transmitter pin of the UART communication.
- RX: It is the receiver pin of UART communication.
- STATE: It designates whether the module is connected or not. It acts as a status bespeaker.

IoT - Platform

As in IoT, all the IoT contrivances are connected to other IoT contrivances and application to transmit and receive information utilizing protocols. There is a gap between the IoT contrivance and IoT application. An IoT Platform fills the gap between the contrivances (sensors) and application (network). Thus we can verbalize that an IoT platform is an integrated accommodation that consummates the gap between the IoT contrivance and application and offers you to bring physical object online.

There are several IoT Platforms available that provides facility to deploy IoT application actively. Some of them are listed below:

Amazon Web Accommodations (AWS) IoT platform: Amazon Web Accommodation IoT platform offers a set of accommodations that connect to several contrivances and maintain the security as well. This platform accumulates data from connected contrivances and performs authentic-time actions.

Microsoft Azure IoT platform: Microsoft Azure IoT platform: offers vigorous security mechanism, scalability and facile integration with systems. It utilizes standard protocols that support bi-directional communication between connected contrivances and platform. Azure IoT platform has an Azure Stream Analytics that processes a substantial magnitude of information in authentic-time engendered by sensors. Some prevalent features provided by this platform are:

A rules engine

- Device shadowing
- Identity registry

Google Cloud Platform IoT: Google Cloud Platform is an ecumenical cloud platform that provides a solution for IoT contrivances and applications. It handles a substantial amplitude of data utilizing Cloud IoT Core by connecting sundry contrivances. It sanctions to apply BigQuery analysis or to apply Machine learning on this data. Some of the features provided by Google Cloud IoT Platform are:

- Cloud IoT Core
- Speed up IoT contrivances
- Cloud publisher-subscriber
- Cloud Machine Learning Engine

IBM Watson IoT platform: The IBM Watson IoT platform enables the developer to deploy the application and building IoT solutions expeditiously. This platform provides the following accommodations:

- Real-time data exchange
- Device management
- Secure Communication
- Data sensor and weather data accommodations

Artik Cloud IoT platform: Arthik cloud IoT platform is developed by Samsung to enable contrivances to connect to cloud accommodations. It has a set of accommodations that perpetually connect contrivances to the cloud and commence accumulating data. It stores the incoming data from connected contrivances and amalgamates this information. This platform contains a set of connectors that connect to third-party accommodations.

Bosch IoT Suite:

Bosch cloud IoT Suit is predicated on Germany. It offers safe and reliable storing of data on its server in Germany. This platform fortifies full app development from archetype to application development.

How IoT platform avail:

- IoT Platform connects sensors and contrivances.
- IoT platform handles different software communication protocol and hardware.

- IoT platform provides security and authentication for sensors and users.

It amasses, visualizes, and analyzes the data amassed by the sensor and contrivance.

ThingWorx in Internet of Things

The ThingWorx platform is a plenary terminus-to-end technology platform that is designed for industrial IoT. It facilitates the implements and accommodations that are required to develop and set-up connectivity, analysis, engenderment of other aspects of IoT development.

The ThingWorx IoT platform is an accumulation of modules that distribute the flexibility, capability, and limberness establishment required to implement IoT applications. ThingWorx potentiates businesses to develop and deploy potent applications expeditiously and augmented authenticity (AR) experiences.

ThingWorx is the first platform that connects the people, systems, things, connection operations, connected products, connected applications, etc. ThingWorx minimizes the time, cost, and jeopardize which are required to build the IoT applications. It deploys the application 10-time more expeditious with model-predicated development.

ThingWorx sanctions you to deploy how you like by providing the consummate application design, runtime, and perspicacious environment. The ThingWorx IoT platform additionally has flexibility and scalability to habituate that application in future.

Accommodations of the ThingWorx platform in IoT

Following are the accommodations and benefits provided by ThingWorx in IoT:

Reason Constructed Platform

This platform specially designed to provide the functionality for the auspice as well as the scalability to develop as the commercial enterprise expands.

Development, Expeditious Amelioration, and Extensibility

It includes a platform module that converges with the ThingModel. The ThinkModel is a veracious digital illustration of items that enables experience, studies, and expeditious apps distribution without any arduousness.

Flexibility

The ThingWorx platform has the flexibility to be deployed on-premises, inside the cloud or a hybrid or both of these platforms.

Component of ThingWorx

ThingWorx offers several key components for application building. This component includes Composer, Mashup builder, storage, search engine, collaboration, and connectivity. The Composer provides a modeling environment for designing , and testing. The Mashup builder is utilized for dashboard building through mundane components such as buttons, lists, wikis, gauges, etc. ThingWorx utilizes a search engine kenned as SQUEAL, for search, query, and analysis.

CHAPTER FIVE

IoT Projects

IoT Project Conceptions

We live in an enthusing age of technological and digital revolution. In just a decennium, we've witnessed a radical vicissitude in the world around us. Thanks to the recent advancements in Data Science, today, we have at our disposal things like AI-powered keenly intellective auxiliaries, autonomous cars, surgical bots, perspicacious cancer detection systems, and of course, the Internet of Things (IoT). So, if you are an abecedarian, the best thing you can do is work on some authentic-time IoT project conceptions.

Essentially, IoT describes a connected network comprising of multiple physical objects that have sensors and perspicacious software embedded in them to facilitate the exchange of data among them via the Internet. However, IoT isn't just circumscribed to everyday household objects – you can even connect sophisticated industrial objects and systems over an IoT network. As of now, there are over 7 billion IoT contrivances, and this number is expected to grow to 22 billion by 2025!

An IoT network leverages an amalgamation of mobile, cloud, and Sizably voluminous Data technologies along with data analytics and low-cost computing to enable the accumulation and exchange of data among physical objects connected within the network. And what's impressive is that all of this is accomplished with minimal human intervention.

As you commence working on IoT project conceptions, you will not only be able to test your strengths and impuissances, but you will withal gain exposure that can be immensely subsidiary to boost your vocation. In this tutorial, you will find intriguing IoT project conceptions for abecedarians to get hands-on experience.

As the IoT technology perpetuates to gain momentum in the modern industry, researchers and tech enthusiasts are yarely investing in the development of pioneering IoT projects. In this post, we'll verbalize about some of the best IoT project conceptions.

IoT Projects Conceptions

This list of IoT project conceptions for students is suited for tyros, and those just starting out with IoT in general. These IoT project conceptions will get you going with all the practicalities you require to prosper in your vocation.

Further, if you're probing for IoT project conceptions for final year, this list should get you peregrinated. So, without further ado, let's jump straight into some IoT project conceptions that will reinforce your base and sanction you to climb up the ladder.

1. Perspicacious Agriculture System

One of the best conceptions to commence experimenting you hands-on IoT projects for students is working on astute agriculture system. As the denomination suggests, this IoT-predicated project fixates on developing a perspicacious agricultural system that can perform and even monitor a host of farming tasks. For instance, you can schedule the system to irrigate a piece of land automatically, or you can spray fertilizers/pesticides on the crops wirelessly through your smartphone.

Not just that, this IoT-predicated project can additionally prosperously monitor soil moisture. Such an advanced system can handle the routine agricultural tasks, thereby sanctioning farmers and cultivators to fixate on more manual-intensive agricultural tasks.

2. Weather Reporting System

This is one of the excellent IoT project conceptions for tyros. This IoT-predicated weather reporting system is concretely designed to facilitate the reporting of weather parameters over the Internet. This is one of the best IoT projects where the system is embedded with temperature, sultriness, and rain sensors that can monitor the weather conditions and provide live reports of weather statistics.

It is an always-on, automated system that sends data via a microcontroller to the webserver utilizing a WIFI connection. This data is updated live on the online server system. So, you can directly check the weather stats online without having to rely on the reports of weather forecasting agencies. The system withal sanctions you to set threshold values and alerts for concrete instances and notifies users every time the weather parameters cross the threshold value.

3. Home Automation System

Home automation is perhaps the most verbalized of IoT projects. IoT-predicated home automation project aims to automate the functioning of household appliances and objects over the Internet. All the household objects that are connected over the IoT network can be controlled and operated through your smartphone.

This is not only convenient but withal gives more power to the utilizer to control and manage household appliances from any location in the world.

This IoT-predicated project utilizes a physical contact-predicated home automation system. The components of this project include a WiFi connection, an AVR family microcontroller, inbuilt touch sensing input pins. While the microcontroller is integrated with the WiFi modem to obtain commands from the utilizer via the Internet, an LCD screen exhibits the system status. When the microcontroller receives a command, it processes the injuctive authorizations to operate the load accordingly and show the system status on an LCD screen.

However, withal Blockchain IoT sanctions homeowners to manage the habitation security system remotely from the smartphone. Mentioning IoT projects can avail your curriculum vitae look much more intriguing than others.

4. Face Apperception Bot

This IoT project involves building an astute AI bot equipped with advanced facial apperception capabilities. This is one of the best IoT Projects where the astute AI bot is designed to apperceive the faces of different people or a single person and withal their unique voice.

The system includes facial apperception features like face detection (perceives faces and attribute the same in an image), person identification (matches an individual in your private repository containing hundreds and thousands of people), and withal emotion apperception (detects a range of countenances including jubilance, contempt, neutrality, and fear).

This amalgamation of advanced apperception features makes for a robust security system. The system additionally includes a camera that lets users preview live streams through face apperception.

5. Perspicacious Garage Door

Affirmative, you can utilize IoT technology to control and operate your garage door! The IoT-predicated astute garage door eliminates the desideratum for carrying bulky keychains. All you require is to configure and integrate your smartphone with the abode IoT network, and you can effortlessly open or close your garage door with just a few clicks of a button.

This perspicacious garage door system incorporates laser and voice commands and astute notifications for monitoring purposes, and withal IFTT integration that sanctions you to engender custom commands for Google Assistant. The astute notification option can trigger alerts in authentic-time to notify as and when the garage door opens or closes, which is a nifty additament. This is one of the most straightforward IoT project conceptions for you to work on.

6. Keenly intellective Alarm Clock

This is one of the fascinating IoT project conceptions. This IoT-predicated alarm clock functions not only as an alarm clock to wake you up every morning, but it can convert into a plenarily-functional contrivance capable of performing other tasks as well. The features of this perspicacious alarm clock include:

- Voice command option to execute standard commands and withal to initiate a video chat.
- A text-to-verbalization synthesizer
- Automatic exhibit refulgence adjustment
- Audio amplifier volume control
- Alphanumeric screen for displaying text

Apart from these features, you can supplementally integrate customizable features on the keenly intellective alarm clock. Fascinatingly enough, the alarm clock offers three ways of waking you up – by playing local mp3 files, by playing tunes from the radio station, and by playing the latest news updates as podcasts.

7. Air Pollution Monitoring System

One of the best conceptions to commence experimenting you hands-on IoT projects for students is working on Air pollution monitoring system. Air pollution is a menace in all components of the world, and monitoring air pollution levels is a challenge that we're facing. While traditional air pollution monitoring systems fail to monitor air pollution levels prosperously and the contaminants, IoT-predicated air pollution monitoring systems can both monitor the caliber of air pollution in cities and preserve the data on web servers for future use.

This astute air pollution monitoring system promotes a cost-efficient technique of determining air quality. The system is embedded with sensors that specially monitor five components of the Environmental Bulwark Agency's Air Quality Index – ozone, carbon monoxide, sulfur dioxide, nitrous oxide, and particulate matter. Plus, the system supplementally includes a gas sensor that can alert users in case of gas leaks or the presence of flammable gases. Apart from this, there's adscititiously a temperature and sultriness sensor.

8. Perspicacious Parking System

With cities and urban areas getting crowded by the minute, finding a parking space is nothing short of a challenge. It is not only time-consuming but adscititiously quite frustrating. Thanks to IoT, there's a solution for solving the parking quandary crisis. This IoT-predicated astute parking system is designed to evade dispensable travelling and harassment in the search for a congruous parking area. This is an excellent IoT projects for neophytes.

So, if you are at a parking space, this system utilizes an IR sensor to monitor the entire area during the run time and provide you an image for equipollent. This sanctions you to visually perceive any free spaces in the parking lot and drive straight to it without wasting any time in probing for a parking space. Withal, the system is tuned to open the car gate n only if there are vacuous slots available in a parking space.

9. Perspicacious Traffic Management System

As the population increases, the number of conveyances plying on the road adscititiously increases ineluctably. Due to the ever-incrementing number of both public and private cars in cities and metropolitan areas, traffic congestion has become a circadian quandary. One of the needed and best IoT projects. To combat this quandary, this IoT-predicated project engenders an astute traffic management system that can efficaciously manage traffic on roads, and offer free pathways to emergency conveyances like ambulance and fire trucks.

Emergency conveyances can connect to this astute system and find signals and pathways where the traffic flow can be controlled dynamically. It flashes a green notification light for emergency conveyances. Supplementally, this astute traffic management system can identify and monitor traffic contraveners even at night.

10. Astute Cradle System

The whole concept behind engendering the astute cradle is to enable parents to check up on their infants and monitor their activities from afar (remote locations).

This is one of the intriguing IoT project conceptions. The IoT-predicated astute cradle system includes a cry detecting mechanism and live-video surveillance along with a utilizer interface (for mobile or web). The cradle is equipped with multiple sensors that can check and monitor the sultriness and temperature of the bed. On the other hand, the surveillance camera affixed to the cradle will perpetuate to send footage of the infant to the parents.

The data engendered by the sensors is stored in the cloud. Adscititiously, the system includes a health algorithm that victuals on the sensor data to perpetually check the health condition of the infant and alert the parents if it senses anything unwonted in the baby's health stats.

11. Astute Gas Leakage Detector Bot

Gas pipes are an indispensable component of both homes and industrial companies. Any leakage in gas pipes can lead to fire accidents and supplementally contaminate the air with pollutants, thereby causing a disastrous effect in the air and the soil. This IoT-predicated project is explicitly built to combat the issue of gas leakage.

This diminutive bot includes a gas sensor that can detect any gas leaks in a building. All you have to do is insert the bot into a pipe, and it will monitor the condition of the pipe as it moves forward. This is one of the consequential and best IoT projects. In case the bot detects any gas leak in the pipeline, it will transmit the location of the leakage in the pipe via an interface GPS sensor over the IoT network. The bot uses IOTgecko to receive and exhibit any gas leakage alert and its location over the IoT network.

12. Streetlight Monitoring System

Streetlights are a consequential source of energy consumption. Often, streetlights perpetuate to remain on even when there's no one in the street. With the avail of this IoT-predicated streetlight monitoring system, we can efficiently monitor and optimize the energy consumption of streetlights.

In this IoT-predicated project, street lights are fitted with LDR sensors that can monitor the kineticism of humans or conveyances in the street. If the sensor can catch any kineticism in the street, it signals the microcontroller, which then turns on the street light. Similarly, if there's kineticism in the street, the microcontroller switches the lights off. This way, a substantial magnitude of energy can be preserved. This is one of the best IoT projects for safety.

Not just that, the astute light system supplementally sanctions users to monitor the estimated power consumption predicated on the current intensity of a streetlight. It is incorporated with a load sensing functionality that can detect any fault in the lights. If the system detects an error, it automatically flags a particular light as faulty and sends the data over to the IoT monitoring system so that it can be fine-tuned promptly.

13. Perspicacious Anti-Larceny System

Security is one of the primary culls for homes, businesses, and corporations. Having a robust security system avails to keep unwanted intruders at bay. The IoT-predicated anti-larceny system is the impeccable solution for safeguarding homes as well as industrial enterprises.

This IoT-predicated security system is programmed to monitor the entire floor of the building for tracking any kind of eccentric kineticism. When turned on, a single kineticism could trigger an alarm, thereby alerting the owners of the property about unwanted visitors. It works something like this – whenever you vacate a house or a building, the Piezo sensor is turned on for tracking any kineticism in and around the property. This is one of the best IoT projects to practice.

So if an intruder were to enter the property, the sensor would send the data to the microcontroller, which then converts it into a signal for the camera to snap a picture of the intruder. This picture is then automatically sent to the users on their smartphone. Mentioning IoT projects can avail your curriculum vitae look much more intriguing than others.

14. Liquid Level Monitoring System

This IoT-predicated project involves building a liquid level monitoring system that can remotely monitor a particular liquid's level and obviate it from overflowing. This project holds immense value for the industrial sector that utilizes sizably voluminous volumes of fluids in their day-to-day operations. Apart from detecting a liquid's level, this monitoring system can additionally be habituated to track the utilization of concrete chemicals and to detect leaks in pipelines.

The system is fitted with ultrasonic, conductive, and float sensors. A WiFi module avails connect the system with the Internet and facilitates data transmission. Four ultrasonic sensors avail transmit the data on the liquid level and alert the utilizer on identically tantamount.

15. Night Patrol Robot

This is one of the best IoT project conceptions. It is a well-established fact that a majority of malefactions occur in the dark, at night. This IoT project aims to develop a patrolling robot that can sentinel your habitation and property at night to obviate and minimize the possibilities of malefactions.

The patrol robot is equipped with a night vision camera with the avail of which it can perform a 360-degree scan of a predefined path. It will scan a particular area, and if it detects human faces and forms of kineticism, it will trigger an alarm to alert the utilizer. The camera of the patrol robot can capture an intruder's image and send the data to the utilizer. The robot can function in a self-adequate manner, without requiring you to hire security sentinels to forfend your habitation.

16. Health Monitoring System

This is one of the intriguing IoT project conceptions to engender. This IoT-powered health monitoring system is designed to sanction patients to take charge of their own health actively. The system will enable users to monitor their body vitals and send the data to qualified medicos and healthcare professionals. The medicos can then provide patients with immediate solutions and guidance predicated on their health condition. The sensors in the application can monitor patient vitals like blood pressure, sugar level, and heartbeat. If the vital stats are higher/lower than conventional, the system will immediately alert the medico.

The conception behind engendering this system is to sanction patients and medicos to connect remotely for the exchange of medical data and expert supervision. You can utilize this application from any location in the world. It is an Arduino-predicated project – the communication occurs between the Arduino platform and an Android app via Bluetooth.

17. Perspicacious Irrigation System

Often, farmers have to irrigate the land manually. Not only is this a time-intensive task, but it is additionally labor-intensive. After all, it is quite challenging for farmers to perpetually monitor the moisture level of the whole field and sprinkle the pieces of land that require dihydrogen monoxide. This IoT project is an astute irrigation system that can analyze the moisture level of the soil and the climatic conditions and automatically dihydrogen monoxide the field as and when required.

You can utilize the keenly intellective irrigation system to check the moisture level, set a predefined threshold for an optimum moisture level of soil, on reaching which the potency supply will get cut-off. An Arduino/328p microcontroller controls the motor that supplies dihydrogen monoxide, and there's an on/off switch with which you can commence or stop the motor. The keenly intellective irrigation system will automatically stop if it commences raining.

18. Flood Detection System

Floods are a mundane natural disaster that occurs virtually every year in our country. Floods not only eradicate agricultural fields and engender, but they additionally take a paramount toll on life. This is why early flood detection is profoundly vital to avert the loss of life and valuable assets.

This IoT-predicated flood detection system is built to monitor and track different natural factors (sultriness, temperature, dihydrogen monoxide level, etc.) relish to prognosticate a flood, thereby sanctioning us to take the obligatory measures for minimizing the damage caused. This IoT Projects uses sensors to accumulate the data for all the pertinent natural factors. For instance, a digital temperature sultriness sensor detects the fluctuations in sultriness and temperature. On the other hand, a float sensor perpetually monitors the dihydrogen monoxide level.

19. Mining Worker Safety Helmet

This is one of the intriguing IoT project conceptions. Mining workers work under prodigiously hazardous and hazardous conditions. Underground environments are plenary of jeopardies, so there is always a trepidation of unpleasant accidents for miners. This mining worker safety helmet utilizes a microcontroller-predicated circuit to track the mining site's environment and evaluate the safety of the workers.

The safety helmet is equipped with an RF-predicated tracking system that avails transmit the data over the IoT network. An atmega microcontroller-predicated RF tracker circuit receives the data that is sent by the helmet nodes. Predicated on this data, the system maps the current location of workers in authentic-time as they move through the mining site.

The helmet additionally includes a panic (emergency) button. If you press this button, an emergency sign will emerge over the IoT web interface. This will alert the management to take the compulsory steps for ascertaining the workers' safety.

20. Keenly intellective Energy Grid

At present, energy grids are not optimized. Often when the electricity grid of a given region fails, the entire area suffers a blackout. This customarily obstructs the quotidian activities of people. This is one of the best IoT project conceptions which proposes a solution to rectify this issue by engendering an astute electricity grid.

This IoT-predicated keenly intellective energy grid utilizes an ATmega family controller to monitor and control the system activities. It utilizes WiFi technology to communicate over the Internet via the IoTGecko webpage. This astute grid's primary task is to facilitate the transmission line's re-connection to an active grid in case a particular grid fails.

So, if an energy grid becomes faulty, the system will switch to the transmission lines of another energy grid, thus, maintaining an uninterrupted electricity supply to the concrete region whose energy grid failed. The system uses two bulbs to designate valid and invalid users. Registered personnel can authenticate in to the IoTGecko webpage and view updates on which grid is active and faulty. This is one of the best IoT Projects to integrate to your curriculum vitae.

CHAPTER SIX

IoT Management

IoT contrivance management refers to the processes involving the provisioning and authenticating, configuring, maintaining, monitoring and diagnosing connected contrivances operating as a component of an IoT environment to provide and support the whole spectrum of their functional capabilities. It is ergo quite pellucid that a reliable and efficacious contrivance management solution is critical in keeping the astute assets connected, au courant and secure.

Now that we have a fairly broad picture of what it betokens to manage the Internet of Things contrivances in terms of business, another step is to grasp why it genuinely matters to any IoT enterprise.

Why contrivances matter?

It's been three decenniums since the first contrivance was connected to the web and browned its first astute piece of toast, and surely the Internet of Things has gone a long way from its humble commencements, and all this incredibly expeditiously. But despite all the promising signs, there is a sense that the Internet of Things is still more of a daydream than the genuine Thing, and there is some evidence indeed to corroborate this.

But the quandary, however marginal it may be, does not lie in the concept itself – it is rather the pace of ecumenical magnification and the rate of technological adaptation that limit the expansion of IoT. In other words, while the Internet of Things wants to hurdle through our businesses and homes like a sprinter, it's still wearing its too tight shoes of technology that painfully curb its velocity and, infrequently, make it stumble along the way.

Ergo, a sturdy and steady evolution of IoT contrivance management is the key factor in bridging the gap between the welkin-rocketing prospects for magnification and the hard authenticity of failing IoT projects and innovative implementations that don't quite hit the mark. But for this to come veridical, the involution and effort of the many IoT accommodation providers and tech visionaries is not enough – it supplementally takes the stakeholders' and entrepreneurs' vigilance of the fundamentals of IoT contrivance management to make apprised decisions about the software solutions they optate for their IoT enterprises.IoT contrivance management fundamentals

For the contrivances to authentically matter, they require to be handled according to some accepted standards and best practices that make up the fundamentals of the management of the Internet of Things contrivances. Getting acquainted with the ropes of the process not only facilitates the decision-making process within the IoT project, but supplementally gives wider vigilance of what transpires with a connected contrivance throughout the whole of its lifecycle.

There are billions of keenly intellective contrivances already up and running in the Internet ecumenical, but every single one of them had to be connected to the web for the very first time. And this process of enrollment into the system is crucial not only in the early stages of the project to avail kickstart the whole enterprise. Astute and secure provisioning expedites time-to-market and circumvents risks cognate to bellicose attacks. If overlooked, it may have astringent consequences for project prosperity.

An indispensable part of provisioning is contrivance authentication. It consists in establishing a secure connection between the contrivance and an IoT accommodation or IoT platform. As a component of that process, the contrivance presents the credentials to the server and, in case it can be trusted, receives further configuration data. Depending on the specifics of the implementation, details of the process may vary, but customarily include authentication methods such as contrivance certificates or pre-shared keys.

As anon as a contrivance gets onboarded, it cannot be left to its resources, as in a "fire and forget" scenario. In most cases keenly intellective contrivances, sensors or other Internet-connected gear comes with generic preconfiguration provided by their manufacturers. This designates that it is up to the accommodation provider to configure the fleet according to the specificity of the deployment, such as the devices' installation location and the role they will play within the emerging IoT ecosystem.

Consequently, one of the key factors in prosperous management of IoT assets is to be able to fine-tune the provisioned contrivances beyond their default settings. Of course, you optate your contrivances to deport precisely how they are intended to comport within the scope of your project – a flexible and intuitive configuration mechanism should enable you to design the comportment of your keenly intellective fleet not only in times when contrivances perform as orchestrated, but withal to react on-the-fly in case of any failures that come along the way.

Verbalizing about fleet, this is the point where contrivance grouping capabilities come into play. Adjusting contrivance settings one after another sounds like a tedious modicum of work. How about the possibility to group the contrivances automatically and according to your desiderata? Indeed, contrivance grouping capabilities are an essential point in any self-reverencing IoT deployment.

With maintenance, we come to another vital point in our list. Unless you're authentically out of touch with the genuine world, you optate to be on top of your connected things. You have them securely provisioned and duly configured, so is there anything else to consider? We have to be cognizant that firmware may come with bugs in it, or, that the project scope may change and incipient functionalities will come in handy, or, that security susceptibilities may appear that pose a threat to your astute deployment. To avail with all of this, comprehensive IoT contrivance management software offers advanced mechanisms for firmware over-the-air and software over-the-air updates, so that every contrivance in the field is kept secure, au courant and bug-free. To learn more about this particular topic, please visit our blog posts on FOTA and SOTA.

Diagnostic features are perhaps the unsung hero of the IoT contrivance management. Firstly, because they are genuinely crucial in truncating the impact of contrivance downtime that may occur as a result of firmware bugs or any unexpected operational issues. Secondly, because they are perhaps as serviceable as they are neglected as a factor in prosperous IoT contrivance management. Fixating on the more conspicuous elements (such as those mentioned above), IoT project managers incline to forget that predictive maintenance can efficaciously preserve the day for their business.

But how is it done? Diagnostics is not only about monitoring network statistics to detect any security breaches; first of all, it's about averting failures from transpiring or counteracting them afore they become deleterious. Taking the whole thing to a higher caliber, IoT contrivance management often uses sophisticated analytics mechanisms for engendering serviceable insights into issues that may pop up across the whole of your IoT deployment.

Now that your fleet has been up and running, opportunely configured and fine-tuned to your utilization case, with its firmware kept au courant and bullet-proof against deplorable actor endeavors and arbitrary failures, you may sit back and relax while your well-oiled IoT machine does all the compulsory work. But there's one inconspicuous yet fundamental aspect still left to consider. Cerebrating about any IoT enterprise in a broader picture, what must be taken into account is what transpires with all the contrivances in the field after the prosperous completion of the project or with a single contrivance when it reaches its terminus of life.

Conspicuously, such assets must be decommissioned, but less conspicuously, this must be done in a cost-efficacious and secure manner. In case of contrivance supersession, a congruous environment should be granted for the deployment of incipient contrivances. When it comes, on the other hand, to phasing out an astute project, the decommissioning efforts should be opportunely orchestrated to eschew data leaks, system downtimes and situations of lamentable agents gaining access to the contrivances due to a system compromise. As can be optically discerned, in being a security matter, terminus of life management is an essential part of handling perspicacious contrivances throughout their lifecycle – visually perceive our blogpost on IoT Contrivance Lifecycle Management for more.

Other Key Considerations

Limpidly, the presented essentials can be perceived not only as guidelines for magnification, but additionally as challenges that can obstruct the prosperous implementation of an IoT system and its connected contrivances, including security, interoperability, power/processing capabilities, scalability, and availability. Many of these can be addressed by an efficacious IoT contrivance management platform, preferably one that adopts widely accepted industry standards.

If considered as such, a well-designed contrivance management avails companies to integrate, organize, monitor and remotely manage contrivances to the Internet at scale, providing critical features to maintain the health, IoT connectivity and security of IoT contrivances throughout their lifecycle.

But contrivance management is not only about the infrastructure, connectivity and software that is utilized to operate the contrivances – it's withal about the IoT protocols, the languages that they 'speak' when communicating. And as the Internet of Things is plagued with immensely colossal lack in standardization in any vertical of IoT technology stack, it is paramount to accentuate the role of such well-established protocols as the Lightweight M2M. As a leading IoT industry standard, LwM2M offers a comprehensive model for Internet of Things contrivance management, designed especially to leverage the possibilities of resource-constrained assets, such as sensors and actuators, which are so vital to the development of the IoT industry ecumenical.

Reaching the Shore of IoT Contrivance Management

In times of incrementing demand for IoT contrivance management solutions, the Internet of Things is indubitably on the ascending tide. But it is still a long way off the safe harbour of standardization, ecumenical adaptation and apperception as a secure and reliable piece of tech to make things more astute than they customarily are. To make it transpire, IoT contrivance management solutions must evolve, at an adequately expeditious pace, towards a comprehensive and coherent vision of what 'smart' stands for – in terms of cities, agriculture, healthcare, home appliances, cars or machine industry or anything else authentically (forests and wine bottles included) – and what it signifies for their clients, so that the fundamentals are not disoriented along the way.

IoT Contrivance Management Features

- Admin Portal
- Technician Portal
- QoE Dashboard
- Business Perspicacity (BI)
- Big Data Analytics
- Extensive API for customization of vertical applications.

Amicable Technologies offers an App Engenderer module that enables the expeditious and facile generation – and update – of any custom applications without supplemental programming.

The Cordial IoT DM platform is available via private cloud, public cloud, or installed on the customer's premises.

The Building Blocks of an IoT Platform

Contrivance Management is an essential component of any IoT platform.

Generic IoT platforms available on the market typically enable the monitoring of IoT sensors and contrivances, data amassment, and application functions.

Astronomically immense-scale IoT deployments require a more advanced set of features, like the ones offered with Friendly's IoT contrivance management, including:

- Provisioning and authentication
- Configuration and control
- Monitoring and diagnostics
- Software updates and maintenance
- Connectivity management
- Advanced analytic capabilities
- Security

Amicable Technologies is the leading provider of plenarily-featured contrivance management solutions, integrated with sundry third-party providers.

Cordial IoT Contrivance Management Platform vs. other IoT solutions

Cordial One-IoT Contrivance Management Server

The Convivial One-IoT Contrivance Management server is a Java-predicated solution that enables the management of millions of IoT contrivances via standard and proprietary protocols. In integration to the management server, the solution includes modules for the Administrator, Call Center, and Network Manager for QoS Monitoring – as well as an extensive API for facile development of vertical applications per customer's needs.

Friendly's One-IoT Contrivance Management server enables the management of the entire lifecycle of IoT contrivances for any vertical – Energy, Utilities,

Agriculture, Perspicacious Home, Keenly Intellective City, Perspicacious Vending, Healthcare, Security, Manufacturing, Fleet Management, Automotive, Asset Tracking, and more.

Cordial IoT Main Features

- Automated provisioning
- Sensor and gateway management
- Manage multiple protocols on one platform: LwM2M, MQTT, TR-369 USP, OMA-DM, CoAP, and others
- Device diagnostics and rehabilitate
- Remote contrivance configuration
- Group management
- Firmware updates
- Monitoring and data amassment
- Event triggering
- Unified API
- Admin & Technician portals

IoT Data Management and Analytics

Amicable One-IoT enables data amassment and data streaming from any IoT-connected contrivance. Data can be stored locally within the customer premise data warehouse or streamed to the cloud. Streaming connectors, like Kafka, MQTT, Pub/Sub, and RESTful are fortified by Friendly's IoT contrivance management platform.

The Cordial One-IoT engine accumulates and stores data for analytics, including:

- Any contrivance parameter
- Sensor/gateway status on/off
- Battery status
- Telemetry data/sensor data
- Location
- Firmware/software version

The system can trigger events based on policies and rules created by the admin.

CHAPTER SEVEN

IoT Security and Safety

Internet of Things (IoT) refers to a prodigious network that provides an interconnection between sundry objects and keenly intellective contrivances. The three paramount components of IoT are sensing, processing, and transmission of data. Nowadays, the incipient IoT technology is utilized in many different sectors, including the domestic, healthcare, telecommunications, environment, industry, construction, dihydrogen monoxide management, and energy. IoT technology, involving the utilization of embedded contrivances, differs from computers, laptops, and mobile contrivances. Due to exchanging personal data engendered by sensors and the possibility of amalgamating both genuine and virtual worlds, security is becoming crucial for IoT systems. Furthermore, IoT requires lightweight encryption techniques.

Prelude

In recent years, technology sector has kenned a genuine evolution. Furthermore, it has become an indispensable implement in our everyday life. Among these recent technologies, the Internet of Things (IoT) has been ameliorated perpetually and has magnetized more and more people. This magnification has positively impacted many sectors, including convivial security, agriculture, inculcation, dihydrogen monoxide management, house security, keenly intellective grid, and so on. Ergo, the number of connected contrivances is incrementing day after day. According to Strategy Analytics, the connected objects will reach more than 38 billion by the cessation of 2025 and 50 billion by 2030.

IoT is an incipient technology that sanctions the implementation of systems interconnecting several objects, either in the physical or virtual world. In fact, the evolution of the Internet commenced with the engenderment of a simple computer network linking personal computers and then moved on to client-server architecture networks, World Wide Web, e-mail, file sharing, etc. Subsequently, it now reaches a wide area network interconnecting billions of keenly intellective objects, which were embedded in sophisticated systems. Their operation is predicated on sensors and actuators designed for monitoring, controlling, and interacting with the physical environment where they subsist.

Despite many advantages, IoT has three main quandaries that are data amassment, data transmission, and data security. To accumulate data, many sensing implements have been introduced and habituated to the IoT contrivances. For transferring accumulated data, sundry protocols have been developed and acclimated in order to enable to the IoT contrivances to connect to subsisted networks and exchange data. However, for the last one, it does not give the attention that it merits. Consequently, many classic and recent security issues are proximately cognate to the IoT as well as authentication, data security, sanction, etc. Indeed, an impotency in authentication can lead to numerous attacks, including replay attack, Denning–Sacco attack, denial of accommodation attack, password conjecturing attack, etc. On the other hand, the authentication of IoT contrivances throughout heterogonous and interconnected protocols is a great challenge. Moreover, these protocols should take into account issues cognate to constraint of IoT contrivances as well as energy consumption, diminutive recollection size, and low processing capability.

IoT Architecture

The concept "Internet of Things" may be defined as a standard that refers to an immensely colossal network connecting sundry sensors, actuators, and microcontrollers introduced in distinct objects. An immensely colossal number of interconnected equipment such as smartphone, industrial machines, computers, conveyances, medical implements, irrigation system, TVs, or refrigerators can be a component of the IoT . Furthermore, IoT is a rather recent design that stands out from its antecedents, including all traditional, mobile, and sensor-predicated Internet networks. IoT includes a prodigiously and sizably voluminous number of hybrid terminals. Since the majority of these contrivances can be connected to the Internet, they generally support mundane web techniques, including HTTP, JSON, XML, etc. One of the strengths of this technology is that it is well fortified and can ergo be acclimated to different subsisting infrastructures. Furthermore, some incipient protocols are especially considered for IoT, for example, CoAP and MQTT are alternatives to HTTP and 6LoWPAN is withal an alternative of IPv4/IPv6.

Due to non-standardization of IoT, there are sundry architectures that are different. However, it focus here on two kenned ones that are three- and five-layer architectures. As the three-layer architecture consists of three layers including perception, networking, and application layers. The role of each layer is described in the following.(i)The perception layer is the first layer of IoT architecture. It is connected to the physical world for sensing and amassing data from their environment. This layer consists of sensors and actuators to quantify some values such as temperature, pH, light, gas, and so on, and to detect some functionality such as location and kineticism. (ii)The network layer is the second layer; its role is to connect to sundry astute contrivances, gateways, and servers. It is responsible for transferring the captured values to other IoT network components. For these reasons, IoT uses several kinds of communication protocols and norms such as 4G/5G, Wi-Fi, ZigBee, Bluetooth, 6LoWPAN, WiMAX, and so on.(iii)The application layer can offer the concrete accommodation requested by utilizer. For instance, this application can provide medicos some health parameters of patients. This layer determines which applications can be installed, such as keenly intellective environment, astute homes, and dihydrogen monoxide monitoring.

On the other hand, the five-layer architecture includes processing and business layers in additament to the three precedent ones. The five layers are perception, convey, processing, application, and business layers. The responsibilities of perception convey, and application layers are identical to the homogeneous layers in three-layer architecture. The roles of the additament layers are detailed as follows :(i)The processing layer is withal apperceived as the middleware layer. It is responsible for controlling, analyzing, processing, and storing received data. It can make decisions according to the processing data without human intervention. This layer benefits from subsisting solutions including cloud computing, immensely colossal data, and databases.(ii)The business layer has a responsibility to manage the whole IoT systems. So, its role is to control applications, business, and profit models. Furthermore, the users' privacy can be managed by this layer.

Security Issues in IoT

DOS

Denial of service (DOS) is a security attack that aims to prevent legitimate user and entity to have an authorized access to network resources. It is considered as the most popular and dominant attack. Generally, attackers can use flooding attack to exhaust system's resources including memory, CPU, and bandwidth. Thus, he either prevents the system to provide service or he makes it ineffective. In this attack, pirates can use numerous skills such as sending unwanted packets or flooding network with multiple messages. Therefore, legitimate users are prevented from taking advantage of services.

Replay Attack

Replay attack is among old attacks on communication network, especially on authentication and key exchanging protocols. It allows the pirate to capture and store a fragment or the whole of captured session in a legitimate traffic. After gaining the trust in a public network, the attacker either sends the captured message to the entity that has participated in origin session or to another different destination. Therefore, in IoT networks, replay attack is measured as a security weakness in which particular data are stored without any authorization before been sent back to the receiver. The goal of this attack is to trap the person in an unauthorized operation. For example, in a smart home system, a temperature sensor is used to detect the temperature and then the measured values are sent to system controller. Based on these values, the system can run or stop the air conditioner to adapt the air temperature as desired by the personnel. However, if an attacker has pirated the sensor's temperature, he can save the day's values and send them at night. As result, the air conditioner will not be functioning normally.

To deal with replay attack, current solutions use three main mechanisms including timestamp, nonce, and response-challenge. The first one is the mechanism that helps to detect replay attack by checking the freshness of received message. Nonetheless, it is hard to assure time synchronization between IoT objects. The second mechanism is the nonce, which is a series of random digits. However, the problem of this mechanism is that the node has no sufficient memory for keeping the list of received nonces. The last mechanism is the challenge-response. It has as objective to verify that the other party can resolve some challenges. But this technique necessitates that the two entities have a pre shared secret.

Password Guessing Attack

Due to the importance of password in authentication process and its large adoption by numerous authentication protocols, pirates have invented various attacks to get the correct one. Hence, the most used attack is password guessing. Particularly, this attack can be executed either online or offline. In this attack, an attacker eavesdrops on the communication between two entities during authentication phase to get some useful values. Then, attacker must guess all probable passwords to succeed in the authentication.

Spoofing Attack

In the network security context, spoofing attack is a situation when an unauthorized entity produces falsified parameter. The goal of this attack is to make servers believe that the attacker is an authorized entity. So, the pirate gains the trust of the authority. For example, in smart health, the pirate can send fake information to authentication server. So, if he performed the authentication phase successfully, he can request victim's sensor and then get the secret health information about this victim.

Insider Attack

In cyber security field, insider attack occurs when a legitimate entity that has an authorized access tries to harm the system. The action of authorized entity can be either intentional or accidental [80–84]. In both cases, the system is considered vulnerable and we should find out the solution in the short term and more than 57% of confidential business data are targeted by insider attack.

Required Security Services for IoT

After debating various security attacks applied by attackers, this section mentions some security services. Thus, the objective of this section is to discuss the security requirements for IoT devices.

Confidentiality

Generally, confidentiality can be defined as the capability and aptitude to prevent an unauthorized user to access private data. Therefore, it promises and guarantees that the personal information is only consulted, edited, or removed by authorized entity. Particularly, in the Internet of Things network, confidentiality is one of the significant security services. However, the confidentiality is the most attacked service. For example, viruses, spywares, and Trojans are considered as malware applications that attack the confidentiality of the user's private data. They can interact with system as executable codes or scripts with the aim to have an unauthorized access.

In an IoT context, for warranting and assuring the confidentiality of personal information captured by sensors and for preventing them from being discovered by the third party, the encryption algorithms and cryptographic methods can be used. Therefore, all transmitted data between two devices must be encrypted. As a result, nobody can understand the message except legitimate entities.

Availability

An alternative required security service of IoT is the availability of resources to the legitimate entities independent of where and when they exist. Availability denotes that the resources and information must be easily reached by the legitimate user when he wants. Moreover, in the IoT architecture, the sensor is available if it can communicate the sensed values in real time.

Likewise, the availability of an actuator means that it can execute user received commands immediately without any remarkable delay.

The availability of some particular resources could be interrupted as consequences of usage of dissimilar data transmission channel, networks, and protocols. On the other hand, for damaging the availability, attackers may use three main malicious attacks including denial of service (DOS) attack, flooding attack, or black hole attack. For the first one, it is probably practiced in the availability situation. Pirates can use the simple denial of service (DOS) attack or distributed denial of service (DDOS) attack that necessitates the collaboration between various resources. For the flooding attack, the attacker can flood the networks by unwanted messages and commands for exhausting device resources. This attack not only targets bandwidth but also decreases CPU and memory capabilities. So, the device will not be reached or the communication will be slow.

In order to guarantee the availability of appropriate resources, we can select distributed approach for operating the system and use numerous platforms which simplify the incorporation of various systems remotely.

Authentication

Authentication service is considered the biggest challenge in the IoT network. It includes verification of identity. On the one hand, in the authentication procedure, the devices must be able to check the validity and legitimacy of remote use in a public network. On the other hand, authentication prevents unauthorized person to take part in a private secured communication. Previous authentication schemes are based on single factor that is a simple password. However, these schemes have to face various issues related to the password. First of all, users can easily forget the password. Secondly, users may have weak password. Finally, attackers are able to guess the correct password, either using exhaustive research attack or dictionary attack. Accordingly, password-based authentication is not enough to promise security. In our days, authentication schemes based on smart card offer multifactor authentication. Typically, the system requires two factors including a valid smart card and correct preshared secret. Even so, it comprises the use of biometric print.

Due to the important position of authentication mechanism in the Internet of Things security, we have reserved the two following sections for discussing various techniques used for authentication in IoT and for studying some proposed IoT authentication schemes.

Authorization

With the growth of number of connected objects to the Internet network, authorization is becoming a critical issue in the IoT system. In fact, it refers to the security service responsible for determining user right and privileges (read, write, or delete). It identifies also the access control rules to allow or deny permissions to the IoT devices. Thus, the challenge is to prevent users with limited privileges to get additional ones to have an unauthorized access to devices and their data.

Integrity

Integrity means that the message was not reformed by an unauthorized entity in the transmission session. So, it guarantees that the receiver has received exactly what the source has sent. The main objective is to stop an unauthorized object doing illegal modification.

For sustaining the safety of smart devices in IoT network, the system should guarantee data integrity. Therefore, neither unauthorized objects nor user access should be granted. Besides, the cryptography and encryption mechanisms can be applied when the transmitted data are very important. It is suggested the usage of HMAC-SHA 256 algorithm for reassuring data integrity.

Non-Repudiation

Non-repudiation is one of the security aspects, which insures that communication members have ability to send or receive information in its integrality. In addition, it makes confident that the transfer of data or identifications between two IoT objects is undeniable. Non-repudiation guarantees to a source node to send its data, as well as to a receiving node to confirm that the received data are matching with data's source .IoT Authentication Techniques

Due to the ability of IoT to access to all users' information, the user's private life must be protected against the malicious attacks. Furthermore, the devices should not be accessed by unauthorized users. So, it is necessary to check the user's identity before getting the authorization. Hence, the verification of user's identity can be done in many ways. Nevertheless, the most frequently used is authentication system, which is based on the prior sharing secrets, keys, or passwords. Consequently, in this section, we review the techniques that are applied for reinforcing the authentication in IoT environment.

One Time Password Authentication

One time password (OTP) which is also called dynamic password is a password that is valid for authentication in one transaction. In the literature survey, various OTP authentication protocols are proposed for securing the communication in IoT environment. These protocols are founded based on various mechanisms such as time synchronization, hash factions (MD5, SHA1, and SHA256), and cryptography RSA. Besides, they are all based on the OTP algorithm.Unfortunately, these protocols are vulnerable against some attacks.

On the other hand, for reinforcing the OTP authentication, Lee and Kim proposed in 2013 an insider attack-resistant OTP scheme based on bilinear maps. However, it needs complex computation. Based on this problem, the protocol uses the principles of lightweight identity-based elliptic curve cryptography and Lamport's OTP algorithm.

ECC-Based Mutual Authentication

Generally, IoT devices have a limited resources. Besides, the communication between sensors, actuators, objects, and nodes must be in real time. For these reasons, it is indispensable to propose a lightweight authentication protocol for IoT. Accordingly, Azrour et al. an efficient authentication scheme for IoT. This protocol is based on elliptic curve cryptography (ECC) which is measured better than the traditional RSA encryption algorithm. Furthermore, in addition, various authentication protocol based on ECC. Elliptic curve cryptography is considered more efficient and more secure especially for systems with limited memory and processing capabilities.

ID- and Password-Based Authentication

ID-based authentication is an approach for distinguishing authorized entities from illegal ones. According to ID, the user is either allowed or denied to access the resource. User ID refers to all attributes that can characterize one user form another, for instance, username, e-mail, phone number, IP address, etc. In IoT environment, numerous protocols are proposed based on this technique. However, this method is generally adopted in the server/client authentication architecture. In view of that, a server is required in IoT environment for storing user's ID and secret in server's database.

On the other hand, the usage of ID-based authentication approach has some issues that are detailed in following lines. Firstly, how user's data are stored in server? Is the server capable to protect them against stolen verifier attack and insider attack? Secondly, users may forget their authentication parameters. Therefore, they cannot perform the next authentication. In this case, it is not suitable to save personal ID in an electronic device (laptop, tablet, and smartphone), even if it is not connected to public network. Thirdly, the transmission of user ID in public network is another challenge. In this situation, the hash functions or cryptography algorithm are recommended.

Certificate-Based Authentication

For addressing problems of ID- and password-based authentication, an alternative approach was proposed. This technique is called certificate-based authentication. Certificate-based authentication has been commonly adopted by multiple applications. For example, in order to verify user's identity in banking application, A new certificate-based authentication scheme. This approach has been also used in IoT environment. Although certificate-based authentication provides more security, device certificate processing and used algorithms necessitate a high processing resource, which is not always available in IoT devices. As a result, this approach is not suitable for IoT objects.

Block chain

Block chain is a particular sort of database. It is different from a traditional database because of the specific way in which it stores data. Block chains save data in a series of blocks that are then linked to each other. In recent years, different authors have taken advantage of this recent technology to propose authentication protocol for IoT. The sustainability and verification of the data stored in the block chain provide the confidence to use accurately recorded data in the future and at the same time provide transparency, anonymity, and traceability.

Multiple and different authentication methods are used in the IoT environment. As demonstrated in Table 2, the majority of proposed IoT authentication protocols are based on encryption cryptography. In this situation, two types of cryptography are used. The first type is asymmetric encryption algorithm such as ECC, while the second one is symmetric encryption algorithm like AES. Furthermore, the hash functions are utilized in some authentication for hashing essential parameters. Finally, the random numbers are also adopted in certain protocol as they can be used to ensure the freshness of messages.

Appendixes

IoT in Construction

While many don't see the development business as mechanically progressed, the IoT in development isn't as distant as we might suspect. It is something reachable for some project workers. Truth be told, one of your groups might be dealing with a brilliant (i.e., associated) place of work.

The development business confronting usefulness trouble. Many ventures run after some time, over spending plan, and the business is more slow than others at correcting to change and it's costing organizations billions.

Huge tasks are taking up to 20% longer to complete than booked and are up to 80% over financial plan, as indicated by research from McKinsey.

Different ventures, for example, fabricating, car have gone to it and other new advances to assist with opening efficiency development along these lines, it additionally could be the answer for the IoT development organizations.

The land and developments by enormous will be changed into IoT gadgets with this innovation. The articles will be associated with the web and information divided between them. Envision a scaffold speaking with your vehicle to educate you regarding all potential courses you can use to stay away from traffic, this will be shocking.

The IoT has become undeniably more open as the web has opened up to individuals. The expense of associating is diminishing, and numerous gadgets presently have Wi-Fi abilities and sensors incorporated directly into them.

Which job does IoT play in the development business?

Peruse on to discover what the Internet of Things is meaning for the present development industry in exceptional ways.

The Internet of Things utilized in the development business to smooth out processes, diminish squander, increment security, and eventually set aside cash and time. In the development business, IoT is at times alluded to as telematics. The IoT, or telematics, permits individuals to stay up with the latest on significant appraisal data about their hardware, for example, the speed of sitting, tire strain, and GPS following.

To more readily see how IoT capacities in the development business, here are some viable ways that this innovation is entering the development zone.

The Internet of Things (IoT) is changing each feature of the structure – how we occupy them, how we oversee them, and even how we fabricate them. There is an immense climate around the present structures, and no piece of the climate is unaffected.

What IoT Meaning for Construction Technology

The speed at which the advanced scene is changing is enjoyably astounding. This has made digitisation of work area fundamental for associations to stay important in the business. This reality applies to the development business, as they need to accept development innovation to stay pertinent, building website web has assumed the liability of aiding the development area adjust and advance to stay aware of new advances.

Innovations affecting the development innovation

Developments like 5G, building webpage broadband association, and the Internet of Things, have changed the face and capacity of the development business. The Internet of Things, which is a milestone advancement, can be controlled from a focal stage, comprising of sensors and savvy gadgets, that share information with one another, which has made working more secure, effective and more astute, conceivable.

Through the Internet of Things, and other enabling developments, the development business has entered one more phase of digitalisation. Now, very much like the QR code, the Internet of Things devices are an essential sensor, however yet, they are creating state of the art PCs that are intended to execute assignments in the development business, for example, quality checking, far off use observing, fix, gear overhauling, hardware following, development devices, distant activity, and supply renewal.

The utilization of broadband innovation in the building site

Nonstop Robotisation

One of the most famous segments of development application is continuous automation. It involves a few applications like welders and cranes, computerized artisans that utilizes data from the sensor to execute guidelines. It is generally utilized in significant applications where security, trustworthiness, availability, and inertness are of incredible importance.

The business can depend on a web association for building destinations like 5G to promptly settle on choices on a worksite, and to perform machine-controlled or far off undertakings since building locales are erratic and a consistently advancing climate. Combined with mind boggling speed, it will empower those attempting to get to cloud applications and data, which permits different customers to ceaselessly speak with them, regardless of their area.

In spite of the fact that, trust and quality are the center pieces of each Internet of Things applications, nonetheless, they have a high importance in essential applications, for example, the quick and steady data conveyed to robots, which will not be fruitful without using a steady and dependable broadband innovation.

Engineering of Healthcare IoT (HIoT)

The system of the IoT that is applied for medical services applications helps to incorporate the benefits of IoT innovation and distributed computing with the field of medication. It additionally spreads out the conventions for the transmission of the patient's information from various sensors and clinical gadgets to a given medical care organization. The geography of a HIoT is the plan of various parts of an IoT medical care framework/network that are reasonably associated in a medical care climate. An essential HIoT framework contains mostly three parts (Figure 1) like distributer, intermediary, and endorser [2]. The distributer addresses an organization of associated sensors and other clinical gadgets that might work independently or all the while to record the patient's imperative data. This data might incorporate pulse, pulse, temperature, oxygen immersion, ECG, EEG, EMG, etc [1]. The distributer can send this data persistently through an organization to a representative. The specialist is liable for the handling and capacity of the procured information in the cloud. At last, the supporter enjoys the constant observing of the patient's data that can be gotten to and envisioned through a cell phone, PC, tablet, and so forth In this, the distributer can handle these information and give criticism later the perception of any physiological irregularity or debasement in the patient's medical issue. The HIoT acclimatizes discrete parts into a half breed lattice where a particular intention is committed to every part on the IoT organization and cloud in the medical services organization. Since the geography for a HIoT relies upon the medical care interest and application, it is difficult to recommend a general design for HIoT. Various underlying changes have been embraced in the past for a HIoT framework [3-6]. It is significant to rattle off completely related exercises connected with the ideal wellbeing application while planning another IoT-based medical services framework for ongoing patient checking. The accomplishment of the IoT framework relies upon how it is fulfilling the prerequisites of medical services suppliers. Since every illness needs a perplexing system of medical care exercises, the geography should observe the clinical guidelines and steps in the determination methodology.

1. L. M. Dang, M. J. Piran, D. Han, K. Min, and H. Moon, "A survey on internet of things and cloud computing for healthcare," *Electronics*, vol. 8, no. 7, p. 768, 2019.View at: Publisher Site | Google Scholar
2. B. Oryema, "Design and implementation of an interoperable messaging system for IoT healthcare services," in *Proceedings of the 2017 14th IEEE Annual Consumer Communications & Networking Conference (CCNC)*, pp. 45–52, Las Vegas, NV, USA, January 2017.View at: Google Scholar
3. A. Ahad, M. Tahir, and K.-L. A. Yau, "5G-based smart healthcare network: architecture, taxonomy, challenges and future research directions," *IEEE Access*, vol. 7, pp. 100747–100762, 2019.View at: Publisher Site | Google Scholar
4. M. N. Birje and S. S. Hanji, "Internet of things based

distributed healthcare systems: a review," *Journal of Data, Information and Management*, vol. 2, 2020.View at: Google Scholar

5. K. T. Kadhim, "An overview of patient's health status monitoring system based on internet of things (IoT)," *Wireless Personal Communications*, vol. 114, pp. 1–28, 2020.View at: Google Scholar
6. Y. Yuehong, "The internet of things in healthcare: an overview," *Journal of Industrial Information Integration*, vol. 1, pp. 3–13, 2016.View at: Google Scholar
7. Y. Yuehong, "The internet of things in healthcare: an overview," *Journal of Industrial Information Integration*, vol. 1, pp. 3–13, 2016.View at: Google Scholar

9 798885 466400